I0023948

Albert Warren

A Book of favourite modern Ballads

Albert Warren

A Book of favourite modern Ballads

ISBN/EAN: 9783742899651

Manufactured in Europe, USA, Canada, Australia, Japa

Cover: Foto ©Thomas Meinert / pixelio.de

Manufactured and distributed by brebook publishing software
(www.brebook.com)

Albert Warren

A Book of favourite modern Ballads

A BOOK

OF

FAVOURITE MODERN BALLADS

ILLUSTRATED WITH FIFTY ENGRAVINGS,

FROM DRAWINGS BY THE FIRST ARTISTS.

LONDON:

W. KENT & CO. (LATE D. BOGUE), 86, FLEET STREET.

1860.

PREFACE

THE chief aim of the Editor of this volume has been to give a collection of such of the Favourite English Ballads,—written since the commencement of the last century—as best admit of picturesque illustration; and by a combination of the productions of Modern Poets and Modern Painters, to present to the literary world an acceptable Gift-book.

The Poets themselves have, in their lyrical pieces, so often interchanged the words "Songs" and "Ballads," that he has felt himself at liberty to include a few well-known verses which, perhaps, more properly belong to the former class. He offers this explanation, lest he may be charged with departing from the promise of the Title-page.

To those living Authors who have kindly permitted him to enrich the volume with flowers picked from their gardens, and to the Artists, who have so ably assisted him in the adornment of its pages, his thanks are especially due.

J. C.

CONTENTS

CONTENTS.

CONTENTS

ILLUSTRATIONS

The Ornamental Designs by ALBERT H. WARREN.

ILLUSTRATIONS.

Engraved and Printed by EDMUND EVANS.

FAVOURITE MODERN BALLADS

CUMNOR HALL.

The dews of summer-night did fall;
　　The moon, sweet regent of the sky,
Silver'd the walls of Cumnor Hall,
　　And many an oak that grew thereby.

Now nought was heard beneath the skies
　　The sounds of busy life were still
Save an unhappy lady's sighs,
　　That issued from that lonely pile.

"Leicester!" she cried, "is this thy love,
　　That thou so oft hast sworn to me,
To leave me in this lonely grove,
　　Immured in shameful privity?

" No more thou com'st with lover's speed,
    Thy once-beloved bride to see;
But be she 'live or be she dead,
    I fear, stern Earl, 's the same to thee.

" Not so the usage I received,
    When happy in my father's hall;
No faithless husband then me grieved,
    No chilling fears did me appal.

" I rose up with the cheerful morn,
    No lark more blythe, no flower more gay;
And like the bird that haunts the thorn,
    So merrily sung the livelong day.

" If that my beauty is but small,
    Amongst court-ladies all despised,
Why didst thou rend it from that hall,
    Where, scornful Earl, it well was prized?

" And when you first to me made suit,
    How fair I was, you oft would say;
And, proud of conquest, pluck'd the fruit,
    Then left the blossom to decay.

" Yes, now neglected and despised,
    The rose is pale, the lily 's dead;
But he that once their charms so prized
    Is, sure, the cause those charms are fled.

" For know, when sick'ning grief doth prey,
    And tender love 's repaid with scorn,
The sweetest beauty will decay
    What floweret can endure the storm?

"At court, I'm told, is beauty's throne,
   Where every lady's passing rare,
That eastern flowers, that shame the sun,
   Are not so glowing, not so fair:

"Then, Earl, why didst thou leave the beds
   Where roses and where lilies vie,
To seek a primrose, whose pale shades
   Must sicken when those gaudes are by?

"'Mong rural beauties I was one:
   Among the fields wild-flowers are fair:
Some country-swain might me have won,
   And thought my beauty passing rare.

"But, Leicester—or I much am wrong,
   Or 'tis not beauty lures thy vows:
Rather ambition's gilded crown
   Makes thee forget thy humble spouse.

"Then, Leicester, why, again, I plead,
   (The injured surely may repine),
Why didst thou wed a country maid,
   When some fair princess might be thine?

"Why didst thou praise my humble charms,
   And, oh! then leave them to decay?
Why didst thou win me to thy arms,
   Then leave me mourn the livelong day?

"The village-maidens of the plain
   Salute me lowly as I go:
Envious they mark my silken train,
   Nor think a Countess can have woe.

"The simple nymphs! they little know
  How far more happy 's their estate :
To smile for joy, than sigh for woe :
  To be content, than to be great.

CUMNOR HALL.

" How far less blest am I than them,
    Daily to pine and waste with care!
Like the poor plant that, from its stem
    Divided, feels the chilling air.

" Nor, cruel Earl, can I enjoy
    The humble charms of solitude;
Your minions proud my peace destroy,
    By sullen frowns or prating rude.

" Last night, as sad I chanced to stray,
    The village death-bell smote my ear;
They wink'd aside, and seem'd to say,
    'Countess, prepare; thy end is near!'

" And now, while happy peasants sleep,
    Here I sit lonely and forlorn;
No one to soothe me as I weep,
    Save Philomel on yonder thorn.

" My spirits flag, my hopes decay—
    Still that dread death-bell smites my ear
And many a boding seems to say,
    'Countess, prepare; thy end is near!' "

Thus, sore and sad, that lady grieved
    In Cumnor Hall, so lone and drear,
And many a heartfelt sigh she heaved,
    And let fall many a bitter tear.

And ere the dawn of day appear'd
    In Cumnor Hall, so lone and drear,
Full many a piercing scream was heard,
    And many a cry of mortal fear.

CUMNOR HALL.

The death-bell thrice was heard to ring;
  An aerial voice was heard to call;
And thrice the raven flapp'd his wing
  Around the towers of Cumnor Hall;

The mastiff howl'd at village door;
  The oaks were shatter'd on the green;
Woe was the hour,— for never more
  That hapless Countess e'er was seen!

And in that manor now no more
  Is cheerful feast and sprightly ball;
For ever since that dreary hour
  Have spirits haunted Cumnor Hall!

The village-maids, with fearful glance,
  Avoid the ancient moss-grown wall,
Nor ever lead the merry dance
  Among the groves of Cumnor Hall.

Full many a traveller oft hath sigh'd,
  And pensive wept the Countess' fall,
As, wand'ring onwards, he has spied
  The haunted towers of Cumnor Hall.

BLACK-EYED SUSAN.

ALL in the Downs the fleet was moor'd,
  The streamers waving in the wind,
When black-eyed Susan came aboard.—
  "Oh! where shall I my true-love find?
Tell me, ye jovial sailors, tell me true,
If my sweet William sails among the crew."

William, who high upon the yard
  Rock'd with the billow to and fro,
Soon as her well-known voice he heard,
  He sigh'd, and cast his eyes below:
The cord slides swiftly through his glowing hands,
And (quick as lightning) on the deck he stands.

So the sweet lark, high poised in air,
    Shuts close his pinions to his breast,
(If chance his mate's shrill call he hear,)
    And drops at once into her nest.
The noblest captain in the British fleet
Might envy William's lip those kisses sweet.

"O Susan, Susan! lovely dear,
  My vows shall ever true remain;
Let me kiss off that falling tear;
  We only part to meet again.
Change as ye list, ye winds! my heart shall be
The faithful compass that still points to thee.

"Believe not what the landsmen say,
  Who tempt with doubts thy constant mind;
They'll tell thee, sailors, when away,
  In every port a mistress find:
Yes, yes! believe them when they tell thee so,
For thou art present wheresoe'er I go.

"If to fair India's coast we sail,
  Thy eyes are seen in diamonds bright
Thy breath is Afric's spicy gale,
  Thy skin is ivory so white.
Thus every beauteous object that I view
Wakes in my soul some charm of lovely Sue.

"Though battle call me from thy arms,
  Let not my pretty Susan mourn;
Though cannons roar, yet, safe from harms,
  William shall to his dear return.
Love turns aside the balls that round me fly,
Lest precious tears should drop from Susan's eye."

The boatswain gave the dreadful word,
  The sails their swelling bosom spread;
No longer must she stay aboard;
  They kiss'd, she sigh'd, he hung his head.
Her lessening boat unwilling rows to land:
"Adieu!" she cries; and wav'd her lily hand.

EDWIN AND EMMA.

Far in the windings of a vale,
　Fast by a sheltering wood,
The safe retreat of Health and Peace,
　An humble cottage stood:

There beauteous Emma flourish'd fair,
　Beneath a mother's eye;
Whose only wish on earth was now
　To see her bless'd, and die.

The softest blush that Nature spreads
　Gave colour to her cheek:
Such orient colour smiles through heav'n,
　When vernal mornings break.

Nor let the pride of great ones scorn
　This charmer of the plains:
That sun, which bids their diamonds blaze,
　To paint our lily deigns.

Long had she fill'd each youth with love,
　Each maiden with despair;
And though by all a wonder own'd,
　Yet knew not she was fair:

Till Edwin came, the pride of swains,
  A soul devoid of art:
And from whose eye, serenely mild,
  Shone forth the feeling heart.

A mutual flame was quickly caught,
  Was quickly, too, reveal'd;
For neither bosom lodg'd a wish
  That virtue keeps conceal'd.

What happy hours of heart-felt bliss
  Did Love on both bestow!
But bliss too mighty long to last,
  Where Fortune proves a foe.

His sister, who, like Envy form'd,
  Like her in mischief joy'd,
To work them harm, with wicked skill
  Each darker art employ'd.

Her father, too, a sordid man,
  Who love nor pity knew,
Was all unfeeling as the clod
  From whence his riches grew.

Long had he seen their secret flame,
  And seen it long unmov'd:
Then with a father's frown at last
  He sternly disapprov'd.

In Edwin's gentle heart a war
  Of differing passions strove:
His heart, that durst not disobey,
  Yet could not cease to love.

Denied her sight, he oft behind
The spreading hawthorn crept,
To snatch a glance, to mark the spot
Where Emma walk'd and wept.

EDWIN AND EMMA.

Oft, too, on Stanmore's wintry waste,
   Beneath the moonlight shade,
In sighs to pour his soften'd soul,
   The midnight mourner stray'd.

His cheek, where health with beauty glow'd,
   A deadly pale o'ercast:
So fades the fresh rose in its prime,
   Before the northern blast.

The parents now, with late remorse,
   Hung o'er his dying bed;
And wearied Heaven with fruitless vows,
   And fruitless sorrows shed.

" 'Tis past!" he cried: " but, if your souls
   Sweet mercy yet can move,
Let these dim eyes once more behold
   What they must ever love!"

She came, his cold hand softly touch'd,
   And bath'd with many a tear:
Fast falling o'er the primrose pale,
   So morning dews appear.

But oh! his sister's jealous care
   (A cruel sister she!)
Forbade what Emma came to say,
   " My Edwin, live for me!"

Now homeward as she hopeless wept
   The church-yard path along,
The blast blew cold, the dark owl scream'd
   Her lover's funeral song.

Amid the falling gloom of night,
  Her startling fancy found
In every bush his hov'ring shade,
  His groan in every sound.

Alone, appall'd, thus had she pass'd
  The visionary vale
When lo! the death-bell smote her ear,
  Sad sounding in the gale!

Just then she reach'd, with trembling step,
  Her aged mother's door:
"He's gone!" she cried, "and I shall see
  That angel-face no more!

"I feel, I feel, this breaking heart
  Beat high against my side!"—
From her white arm down sunk her head,
  She shiver'd, sigh'd, and died.

LOCHINVAR.

O! YOUNG LOCHINVAR is come out of the west,
Through all the wide border his steed was the best;
And save his good broadsword, he weapons had none,
He rode all unarm'd, and he rode all alone.
So faithful in love, and so dauntless in war,
There never was knight like the young Lochinvar.

He staid not for brake, and he stopp'd not for stone,
He swam the Eske river, where ford there was none;
But ere he alighted at Netherby gate,
The bride had consented, the gallant came late:
For a laggard in love, and a dastard in war,
Was to wed the fair Ellen of brave Lochinvar.

LOCHINVAR.

So boldly he enter'd the Netherby Hall,
Among bride's-men, and kinsmen, and brothers, and all :
Then spoke the bride's father, his hand on his sword,
(For the poor craven bridegroom said never a word,)
"O come ye in peace here, or come ye in war,
Or to dance at our bridal, young Lord Lochinvar?"

" I long woo'd your daughter, my suit you denied ;
Love swells like the Solway, but ebbs like its tide ;
And now am I come, with this lost love of mine,
To lead but one measure, drink one cup of wine.
There are maidens in Scotland more lovely by far,
That would gladly be bride to the young Lochinvar."

The bride kiss'd the goblet : the knight took it up,
He quaff'd off the wine, and he threw down the cup.
She look'd down to blush, and she look'd up to sigh,
With a smile on her lips, and a tear in her eye.
He took her soft hand, ere her mother could bar,—
" Now tread we a measure!" said young Lochinvar.

So stately his form, and so lovely her face,
That never a hall such a galliard did grace ;
While her mother did fret, and her father did fume,
And the bridegroom stood dangling his bonnet and plume ;
And the bride's-maidens whisper'd, " 'Twere better by far
To have match'd our fair cousin with young Lochinvar."

One touch to her hand, and one word in her ear,
When they reach'd the hall-door, and the charger stood near ;
So light to the croupe the fair lady he swung,
So light to the saddle before her he sprung !
" She is won! we are gone, over bank, bush, and scaur ;
They'll have fleet steeds that follow," quoth young Lochinvar.

There was mounting 'mong Graemes of the Netherby clan;
Forsters, Fenwicks, and Musgraves, they rode and they ran:
There was racing and chasing on Canobie Lee.
But the lost bride of Netherby ne'er did they see.
So daring in love, and so dauntless in war,
Have you e'er heard of gallant like young Lochinvar?

JOHN BARLEYCORN.

THERE went three kings into the east,
 Three kings both great and high;
And they have sworn a solemn oath,
 John Barleycorn shall die.

They took a plough and plough'd him down,
 Put clods upon his head;
And they have sworn a solemn oath,
 John Barleycorn was dead.

But the cheerful spring came kindly on,
 And showers began to fall;
John Barleycorn got up again,
 And sore surprised them all.

The sultry suns of summer came,
 And he grew thick and strong;
His head well arm'd with pointed spears,
 That no one should him wrong.

The sober autumn enter'd mild,
 And he grew wan and pale;
His bending joints and drooping head
 Show'd he began to fail.

His colour sicken'd more and more,
 He faded into age;
And then his enemies began
 To show their deadly rage.

They took a weapon long and sharp,
 And cut him by the knee;
Then tied him fast upon a cart,
 Like a rogue for forgery.

They laid him down upon his back,
 And cudgel'd him full sore;
They hung him up before the storm,
 And turn'd him o'er and o'er.

They fill'd up then a darksome pit
 With water to the brim,
And heaved in poor John Barleycorn,
 To let him sink or swim.

They laid him out upon the floor,
 To work him further woe;
And still, as signs of life appear'd,
 They toss'd him to and fro.

They wasted o'er a scorching flame
 The marrow of his bones;
But the miller used him worst of all,
 For he crush'd him between two stones.

And they have taken his very heart's blood,
 And drunk it round and round;
And so farewell, John Barleycorn!
 Thy fate thou now hast found.

THE WOODLAND HALLO.

In our cottage, that peeps from the skirts of the wood,
   I am mistress, no mother have I ;
Yet blithe are my days, for my father is good,
   And kind is my lover, hard by :
They both work together beneath the green shade,
   Both woodmen, my father and Joe ;
Where I've listen'd whole hours to the echo that made
   So much of a laugh or—Hallo !

From my basket at noon they expect their supply,
   And with joy from my threshold I spring ;
For the woodlands I love, and the oaks waving high,
   And Echo that sings as I sing.
Though deep shades delight me, yet love is my food,
   As I call the dear name of my Joe ;
His musical shout is the pride of the wood,
   And my heart leaps to hear the—Hallo !

Simple flowers of the grove, little birds live at ease,
   I wish not to wander from you ;
I'll still dwell beneath the deep roar of your trees,
   For I know that my Joe will be true.

The trill of the robin, the coo of the dove,
Are charms that I'll never forego;
But resting through life on the bosom of love,
Will remember the Woodland Hallo.

HOPE AND LOVE.

One day, through Fancy's telescope,
　　Which is my richest treasure,
I saw, dear Susan, Love and Hope
　　Set out in search of Pleasure:
All mirth and smiles I saw them go:
　　Each was the other's banker;
For Hope took up her brother's bow,
　　And Love, his sister's anchor.

They rambled on o'er vale and hill,
　　They pass'd by cot and tower;
Through summer's glow and winter's chill,
　　Through sunshine and through shower:
But what did those fond playmates care
　　For climate or for weather?
All scenes to them were bright and fair,
　　On which they gazed together.

Sometimes they turn'd aside to bless
   Some Muse and her wild numbers,
Or breathe a dream of holiness
   On Beauty's quiet slumbers.
" Fly on," said Wisdom, with cold sneers :
   " I teach my friends to doubt you ;"
" Come back," said Age, with bitter tears,
   " My heart is cold without you."

When Poverty beset their path,
   And threaten'd to divide them,
They coax'd away the beldame's wrath,
   Ere she had breath to chide them,
By vowing all her rags were silk,
   And all her bitters honey,
And showing taste for bread and milk,
   And utter scorn of money.

They met stern Danger in their way,
   Upon a ruin seated :
Before him kings had quaked that day,
   And armies had retreated :
But he was robed in such a cloud,
   As Love and Hope came near him,
That though he thunder'd long and loud,
   They did not see or hear him.

A gray-beard join'd them, Time by name ;
   And Love was nearly crazy,
To find that he was very lame,
   And also very lazy :
Hope, as he listen'd to her tale,
   Tied wings upon his jacket ;
And then they far outran the mail,
   And far out-sail'd the packet.

And so, when they had safely pass'd
   O'er many a land and billow,
Before a grave they stopp'd at last,
   Beneath a weeping willow:
The moon upon the humble mound
   Her softest light was flinging;
And from the thickets all around
   Sad nightingales were singing.

"I leave you here," quoth Father Time,
   As hoarse as any raven;
And Love kneel'd down to spell the rhyme
   Upon the rude stone graven:
But Hope look'd onward, calmly brave,
   And whisper'd, "Dearest brother,
We're parted on this side the grave,
   We'll meet upon the other."

WITHIN A MILE OF EDINBRO' TOWN.

'Twas within a mile of Edinbro' town,
    In the rosy time of the year;
Sweet flowers bloom'd, and the grass was down,
    And each shepherd woo'd his dear.
        Bonnie Jocky, blythe and gay,
        Kiss'd sweet Jenny making hay;
The lassie blush'd, and frowning cried, "No, no, it will not do;
I cannot, cannot, wonnot, wonnot, monnot buckle to."

Jocky was a wag that never would wed,
　　Though long he had follow'd the lass :
Contented she earn'd and eat her brown bread,
　　And merrily turn'd up the grass.
　　　　Bonnie Jocky, blythe and free,
　　　　Won her heart right merrily :
Yet still she blush'd, and frowning cried, " No, no, it will not do :
I cannot, cannot, wonnot, wonnot, mannot buckle to."

But when he vow'd he would make her his bride,
　　Though his flocks and herds were not few,
She gave him her hand, and a kiss beside,
　　And vow'd she'd for ever be true.
　　　　Bonnie Jocky, blythe and free,
　　　　Won her heart right merrily :
At church she no more frowning said, " No, no, it will not do :
I cannot, cannot, wonnot, wonnot, mannot buckle to."

ALLEN-A-DALE.

ALLEN-A-DALE has no faggot for burning,
Allen-a-Dale has no furrow for turning,
Allen-a-Dale has no fleece for the spinning,
Yet Allen-a-Dale has red gold for the winning.
Come, read me my riddle! come, hearken my tale!
And tell me the craft of bold Allen-a-Dale.

The baron of Ravensworth prances in pride,
And he views his domains upon Arkindale side,
The mere for his net, and the land for his game,
The chase for the wild, and the park for the tame;
Yet the fish of the lake, and the deer of the vale,
Are less free to Lord Dacre than Allen-a-Dale!

Allen-a-Dale was ne'er belted a knight,
Though his spur be as sharp, and his blade be as bright:
Allen-a-Dale is no baron or lord,
Yet twenty tall yeomen will draw at his word;
And the best of our nobles his bonnet will vail,
Who at Rerecross on Stanmore meets Allen-a-Dale.

Allen-a-Dale to his wooing is come;
The mother, she ask'd of his household and home;
"Though the castle of Richmond stands fair on the hill,
My hall," quoth bold Allen, " shows gallanter still:
'Tis the blue vault of heav'n, with its crescent so pale,
And with all its bright spangles !" said Allen-a-Dale.

The father was steel, and the mother was stone;
They lifted the latch, and they bade him be gone:
But loud, on the morrow, their wail and their cry:
He had laugh'd on the lass with his bonny black eye,
And she fled to the forest to hear a love-tale,
And the youth it was told by was Allen-a-Dale!

THERE'S NAE LUCK ABOUT THE HOUSE.

But are ye sure the news is true?
    And are ye sure he's weel?
Is this a time to think o' wark?
    Ye jades, fling by your wheel!

For there' nae luck about the house,
    There's nae luck at a';
There's nae luck about the house,
    When our gudeman's awa'.

Is this a time to think o' wark,
    When Colin's at the door?
Rax down my cloak—I'll to the quay,
    And see him come ashore.

Rise up, and make a clean fireside,
    Put on the mickle pot;
Gie little Kate her cotton gown,
    And Jock his Sunday coat.

Mak' a' their shoon as black as sloes,
    Their stockings white as snaw;
It's a' to pleasure our gudeman
    He likes to see them braw.

THERE'S NAE LUCK ABOUT THE HOUSE

There are twa hens into the crib
 Hae fed this month or mair;
Mak' haste and thraw their necks about,
 That Colin weel may fare.

My Turkey slippers I'll put on,
 My stockings pearl-blue,—
It's a' to pleasure our gudeman,
 For he's baith leal and true.

Sae sweet his voice, sae smooth his tongue,
 His breath's like caller air;
His very foot has music in't,
 As he comes up the stair.

And will I see his face again?
 And will I hear him speak?
I'm downricht dizzy wi' the thought,
 In troth I'm like to greet.

There's nae luck about the house,
 There's nae luck at a';
There's nae luck about the house,
 When our gudeman's awa'.

I REMEMBER

I remember, I remember,
  The house where I was born,
The little window where the sun
  Came peeping in at morn;
He never came a wink too soon,
  Nor brought too long a day,
But now, I often wish the night
  Had borne my breath away!

I remember, I remember,
  The roses, red and white,
The violets, and the lily-cups,
  Those flowers made of light!
The lilacs where the robin built,
  And where my brother set
The laburnum on his birth-day,
  The tree is living yet!

I remember, I remember,
  Where I was used to swing,
And thought the air must rush as fresh
  To swallows on the wing;
My spirit flew in feathers then,
  That is so heavy now,
And summer pools could hardly cool
  The fever on my brow!

I remember, I remember,
　　The fir-trees dark and high,
I used to think their slender tops
　　Were close against the sky:
It was a childish ignorance,
　　But now 'tis little joy
To know I'm farther off from heav'n
　　Than when I was a boy.

THE SAILOR'S JOURNAL.

'Twas post-meridian, half-past four,
  By signal I from Nancy parted:
At six she linger'd on the shore,
  With uplift hands and broken-hearted.
At seven, while taughtening the fore-stay,
  I saw her faint, or else 'twas fancy;
At eight we all got under weigh,
  And bade a long adieu to Nancy!

Night came, and now eight bells had rung,
  While careless sailors, ever cheery,
On the mid-watch so jovial sung,
  With tempers labour cannot weary.
I, little to their mirth inclined,
  While tender thoughts rush'd on my fancy,
And my warm sighs increased the wind,
  Look'd on the moon, and thought of Nancy!

And now arrived that jovial night,
  When every true-bred tar carouses;
When, o'er the grog, all hands delight
  To toast their sweethearts and their spouses.
Round went the can, the jest, the glee,
  While tender wishes fill'd each fancy;
And when, in turn, it came to me,
  I heaved a sigh, and toasted Nancy!

Next morn a storm came on at four,
　　At six, the elements in motion
Plunged me and three poor sailors more
　　Headlong within the foaming ocean.
Poor wretches! they soon found their graves:
　　For me　it may be only fancy,
But Love seem'd to forbid the waves
　　To snatch me from the arms of Nancy!

Scarce the foul hurricane was clear'd,
    Scarce winds and waves had ceased to rattle,
When a bold enemy appear'd,
    And, dauntless, we prepared for battle.
And now, while some loved friend or wife
    Like lightning rush'd on every fancy,
To Providence I trusted life,
    Put up a prayer, and thought of Nancy!

At last,— 'twas in the month of May,
    The crew, it being lovely weather,
At three a.m. discover'd day,
    And England's chalky cliffs together.
At seven, up channel how we bore,
    While hopes and fears rush'd on my fancy;
At twelve I gaily jump'd ashore,
    And to my throbbing heart press'd Nancy!

LORD ULLIN'S DAUGHTER.

A CHIEFTAIN, to the Highlands bound,
  Cries, "Boatman, do not tarry!
And I'll give thee a silver pound
  To row us o'er the ferry."

"Now who be ye, would cross Lochgyle,
  This dark and stormy water?"
"O, I'm the chief of Ulva's isle,
  And this Lord Ullin's daughter:

"And fast before her father's men
  Three days we've fled together;
For should he find us in the glen,
  My blood would stain the heather.

"His horsemen hard behind us ride;
  Should they our steps discover,
Then who will cheer my bonny bride,
  When they have slain her lover?"

Out spoke the hardy Highland wight,
  "I'll go, my chief—I'm ready:
It is not for your silver bright,
  But for your winsome lady:

"And by my word! the bonny bird
  In danger shall not tarry:
So, though the waves are raging white,
  I'll row you o'er the ferry."

By this the storm grew loud apace,
  The water-wraith was shrieking;
And in the scowl of heav'n each face
  Grew dark as they were speaking.

But still, as wilder blew the wind,
  And as the night grew drearer,
Adown the glen rode armed men,
  Their trampling sounded nearer.—

"O haste thee, haste!" the lady cries,
  "Though tempests round us gather;
I'll meet the raging of the skies,
  But not an angry father."

The boat has left a stormy land,
  A stormy sea before her,—
When, oh! too strong for human hand,
  The tempest gather'd o'er her.

And still they row'd, amidst the roar
  Of waters fast prevailing:
Lord Ullin reach'd that fatal shore,
  His wrath was changed to wailing.—

For sore dismay'd, through storm and shade,
  His child he did discover:
One lovely hand she stretch'd for aid,
  And one was round her lover.

"Come back! come back!" he cried in grief,
    " Across this stormy water:
And I'll forgive your Highland chief,
    My daughter!—oh my daughter!"

'Twas vain:—the loud waves lash'd the shore,
    Return or aid preventing;—
The waters wild went o'er his child,
    And he was left lamenting.

THE ANGELS' WHISPER.

A BABY was sleeping, its mother was weeping,
    For her husband was far on the wild raging sea;
And the tempest was swelling round the fisherman's dwelling,
    And she cried, " Dermot, darling, oh! come back to me."

Her beads while she number'd, the baby still slumber'd,
    And smiled in her face while she bended her knee:
" Oh! bless'd be that warning, my child, thy sleep adorning,
    For I know that the angels are whisp'ring with thee.

" And while they are keeping bright watch o'er thy sleeping,
    Oh! pray to them softly, my baby, with me;
And say thou wouldst rather they'd watch'd o'er thy father,
    For I know that the angels are whisp'ring with thee."

The dawn of the morning saw Dermot returning,
    And the wife wept with joy her babe's father to see;
And closely caressing her child, with a blessing,
    Said, " I knew that the angels were whisp'ring with thee."

EDWIN AND ANGELINA.

"Turn, gentle Hermit of the dale,
    And guide my lonely way,
To where yon taper cheers the vale
    With hospitable ray.

"For here, forlorn and lost, I tread,
    With fainting steps and slow;
Where wilds, immeasurably spread,
    Seem lengthening as I go."

"Forbear, my son," the Hermit cries,
    "To tempt the dangerous gloom;
For yonder faithless phantom flies
    To lure thee to thy doom.

"Here to the houseless child of want
    My door is open still;
And, though my portion is but scant,
    I give it with good will.

"Then turn, to-night, and freely share
    Whate'er my cell bestows,—
My rushy couch and frugal fare,
    My blessing and repose.

"No flocks, that range the valley free,
    To slaughter I condemn:
Taught by that Power who pities me,
    I learn to pity them.

" But from the mountain's grassy side
　　A guiltless feast I bring,—
A scrip with herbs and fruits supplied,
　　And water from the spring.

"Then, Pilgrim, turn, thy cares forego:
　　All earth-born cares are wrong:
Man wants but little here below.
　　Nor wants that little long."

Soft as the dew from heav'n descends.
　　His gentle accents fell:
The modest stranger lowly bends.
　　And follows to the cell.

Far, in a wilderness obscure.
　　The lonely mansion lay:
A refuge to the neighbouring poor.
　　And strangers led astray.

No stores beneath its humble thatch
　　Required a master's care;
The wicket, opening with a latch.
　　Received the harmless pair.

And now, when busy crowds retire.
　　To take their evening rest,
The Hermit trimm'd his little fire.
　　And cheer'd his pensive guest:

And spread his vegetable store,
　　And gaily press'd, and smiled;
And, skill'd in legendary lore,
　　The lingering hours beguiled.

Around, in sympathetic mirth,
    Its tricks the kitten tries;
The cricket chirrups in the hearth,
    The crackling faggot flies.

But nothing could a charm impart,
    To soothe the stranger's woe;
For grief was heavy at his heart,
    And tears began to flow.

His rising cares the Hermit spied,
    With answering care opprest:
" And whence, unhappy youth," he cried,
    " The sorrows of thy breast?

" From better habitations spurn'd,
    Reluctant dost thou rove?
Or grieve for friendship unreturn'd,
    Or unregarded love?

" Alas! the joys that fortune brings
    Are trifling and decay:
And those who prize the paltry things
    More trifling still than they.

" And what is friendship but a name,
    A charm that lulls to sleep!
A shade that follows wealth or fame,
    And leaves the wretch to weep!

" And love is still an emptier sound,
    The modern fair-one's jest;
On earth unseen, or only found
    To warm the turtle's nest

" For shame, fond youth, thy sorrows hush,
  And spurn the sex," he said :
But, while he spoke, a rising blush
  His love-lorn guest betray'd.

Surprised he sees new beauties rise,
  Swift mantling to the view,
Like colours o'er the morning skies,
  As bright, as transient too.

The bashful look, the rising breast,
  Alternate spread alarms;
The lovely stranger stands confess'd,
  A maid in all her charms.

"And, ah! forgive a stranger rude,
  A wretch forlorn," she cried,
"Whose feet unhallow'd thus intrude,
  Where Heav'n and you reside.

"But let a maid thy pity share,
  Whom love has taught to stray;
Who seeks for rest, but finds despair
  Companion of her way.

"My father lived beside the Tyne,
  A wealthy lord was he;
And all his wealth was mark'd as mine,—
  He had but only me.

"To win me from his tender arms,
  Unnumber'd suitors came,
Who praised me for imputed charms,
  And felt or feign'd a flame.

"Each hour a mercenary crowd
  With richest proffers strove:
Among the rest young Edwin bow'd,
  But never talk'd of love.

"In humblest, simplest habit clad,
  No wealth nor power had he;
Wisdom and worth were all he had,
  But these were all to me.

" And when, beside me in the dale,
 He caroll'd lays of love,
His breath lent fragrance to the gale,
 And music to the grove.

" The blossom opening to the day,
 The dews of heav'n refined,
Could nought of purity display,
 To emulate his mind.

" The dew, the blossoms on the tree,
 With charms inconstant shine;
Their charms were his; but, woe to me!
 Their constancy was mine.

" For still I tried each fickle art,
 Importunate and vain;
And while his passion touch'd my heart,
 I triumph'd in his pain.

" Till, quite dejected with my scorn,
 He left me to my pride;
And sought a solitude forlorn,
 In secret, where he died!

" But mine the sorrow, mine the fault,
 And well my life shall pay:
I'll seek the solitude he sought,
 And stretch me where he lay.

" And there, forlorn, despairing, hid,
 I'll lay me down and die;
'Twas so for me that Edwin did,
 And so for him will I."

" Forbid it, Heav'n!" the Hermit cried,
 And clasp'd her to his breast:
The wondering fair-one turn'd to chide, —
 'Twas Edwin's self that prest!

"Turn, Angelina, ever dear,
    My charmer, turn to see
Thy own, thy long-lost Edwin here,
    Restor'd to love and thee.

Thus let me hold thee to my heart,
    And ev'ry care resign:
And shall we never, never part,
    My life—my all that's mine?

"No, never from this hour to part,
    We 'll live and love so true:
The sigh that rends thy constant heart
    Shall break thy Edwin's too."

THE LASS OF RICHMOND HILL.

On Richmond Hill there lives a lass
    More bright than May-day morn,
Whose charms all other maids surpass
    A rose without a thorn.

This lass so neat, with smiles so sweet,
    Has won my right good-will;
I'd crowns resign to call her mine,
    Sweet lass of Richmond Hill.

THE LASS OF RICHMOND HILL.

Ye zephyrs gay, that fan the air,
  And wanton through the grove,
Oh! whisper to my charming fair,
  I die for her I love.

How happy will the shepherd be
  Who calls this nymph his own!
Oh! may her choice be fix'd on me,
  Mine's fix'd on her alone.

THE HERMIT.

At the close of the day, when the hamlet is still,
 And mortals the sweets of forgetfulness prove;
When nought but the torrent is heard on the hill,
 And nought but the nightingale's song in the grove;
'Twas then, by the cave of the mountain reclined,
 A Hermit his nightly complaint thus began:
Though mournful his numbers, his soul was resign'd;
 He thought as a sage, though he felt as a man.

THE HERMIT.

" Ah ! why thus abandon'd to darkness and woe ?
    Why thus, lonely Philomel, flows thy sad strain ?
For Spring shall return, and a lover bestow,
    And thy bosom no trace of misfortune retain.
Yet, if pity inspire thee, oh ! cease not thy lay ;
    Mourn, sweetest companion ! man calls thee to mourn :
Oh ! soothe him, whose pleasures, like thine, pass away ;
    Full quickly they pass—but they never return !

" Now, gliding remote on the verge of the sky,
    The moon, half-extinct, a dim crescent displays :
But lately I mark'd, when, majestic on high,
    She shone, and the planets were lost in her blaze.
Roll on then, fair orb, and with gladness pursue
    The path that conducts thee to splendour again :
But man's faded glory no change shall renew ;
    Ah, fool ! to exult in a glory so vain !

" 'Tis night, and the landscape is lovely no more ;
    I mourn ; but, ye woodlands, I mourn not for you ;
For morn is approaching, your charms to restore,
    Perfumed with fresh fragrance, and glitt'ring with dew.
Nor yet for the ravage of Winter I mourn ;
    Kind Nature the embryo blossom shall save :
But when shall Spring visit the mouldering urn ?
    Oh ! when shall it dawn on the night of the grave ? "

EXCELSIOR

THE shades of night were falling fast,
As through an Alpine village pass'd
A youth, who bore, 'mid snow and ice,
A banner with the strange device,
Excelsior!

His brow was sad; his eye beneath
Flash'd like a falchion from its sheath;
And like a silver clarion rung
The accents of that unknown tongue,
Excelsior!

In happy homes he saw the light
Of household fires gleam warm and bright;
Above, the spectral glaciers shone,
And from his lips escaped a groan,
Excelsior!

"Try not the Pass!" the old man said;
"Dark lowers the tempest overhead;
The roaring torrent is deep and wide!"
And loud that clarion voice replied,
Excelsior!

"O stay," the maiden said, "and rest
Thy weary head upon this breast!"
A tear stood in his bright blue eye,
But still he answer'd, with a sigh,
Excelsior!

"Beware the pine-tree's wither'd branch!
Beware the awful avalanche!"
This was the peasant's last good-night,—
A voice replied, far up the height,
   Excelsior!

At break of day, as heavenward
The pious monks of Saint Bernard
Utter'd the oft-repeated prayer,
A voice cried through the startled air,
   Excelsior!

A traveller by the faithful hound
Half-buried in the snow was found,
Still grasping in his hand of ice
That banner with the strange device
   Excelsior!

There, in the twilight cold and gray,
Lifeless, but beautiful, he lay;
And from the sky, serene and far,
A voice came, like a falling star—
   Excelsior!

DUNCAN GRAY.

Duncan Gray cam' here to woo,
    Ha, ha! the wooing o't,
On blythe Yule night when we were fou,
    Ha, ha! the wooing o't.
Maggie coost her head fu' high,
Look'd asklent and unco skeigh,
Gart poor Duncan stand abeigh;
    Ha, ha! the wooing o't.

Duncan fleech'd, and Duncan pray'd,
    Ha, ha! the wooing o't;
Meg was deaf as Ailsa Craig,
    Ha, ha! the wooing o't.
Duncan sigh'd baith out and in,
Grat his een baith bleer't and blin',
Spak' o' lowpin o'er a linn;
    Ha, ha! the wooing o't.

Time and chance are but a tide,
    Ha, ha! the wooing o't;
Slighted love is sair to bide,
    Ha, ha! the wooing o't.
"Shall I, like a fool," quoth he,
"For a haughty hizzie die?
She may gae to—France for me!"
    Ha, ha! the wooing o't.

How it comes let doctors tell,
     Ha, ha! the wooing o't,
Meg grew sick—as he grew heal;
     Ha, ha! the wooing o't.
Something in her bosom wrings,
For relief a sigh she brings;
And oh! her een, they spak' sic things!
     Ha, ha! the wooing o't.

Duncan was a lad o' grace,
     Ha, ha! the wooing o't;
Maggie's was a piteous case,
     Ha, ha! the wooing o't;
Duncan couldna be her death,
Swelling pity smoor'd his wrath;
Now they're crouse and canty baith;
     Ha, ha! the wooing o't.

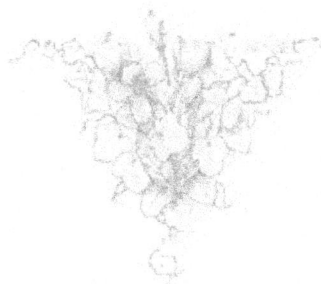

THE FRIAR OF ORDERS GRAY.

It was a friar of orders gray
    Walkt forth to tell his beades ;
And he met with a lady faire
    Clad in a pilgrime's weedes.

" Now Christ thee save, thou reverend friar,
    I pray thee tell to me,
If ever at yon holy shrine
    My true love thou didst see ? "

" And how should I know your true love
    From many another one ? "
" O, by his cockle hat and staff,
    And by his sandal shoone ;

" But chiefly by his face and mien,
    That were so fair to view ;
His flaxen locks that sweetly curl'd,
    And eyne of lovely blue."

" O lady, he is dead and gone !
    Lady, he's dead and gone !
And at his head a green grass turfe,
    And at his heels a stone.

" Within these holy cloysters long
    He languisht, and he dyed,
Lamenting of a ladye's love,
    And 'playning of her pride

" Here bore him bareface on his bier
　　Six proper youths and tall,
And many a tear bedew'd his grave
　　Within you kirk-yard wall."

" And art thou dead, thou gentle youth !
　　And art thou dead and gone !
And didst thou dye for love of me !
　　Break, cruel heart of stone !"

" O weep not, lady, weep not soe :
　　Some ghostly comfort seek :
Let not vain sorrow rive thy heart,
　　Ne teares bedew thy cheek."

" O do not, do not, holy friar,
　　My sorrow now reprove ;
For I have lost the sweetest youth
　　That e'er won ladye's love.

" And nowe, alas ! for thy sad losse,
　　I'll evermore weep and sigh :
For thee I only wisht to live,
　　For thee I wish to dye."

" Weep no more, lady, weep no more,
　　Thy sorrowe is in vaine :
For violets pluckt the sweetest showers
　　Will ne'er make grow againe.

" Our joys as winged dreams doe flye ;
　　Why, then, should sorrow last ?
Since grief but aggravates thy losse,
　　Grieve not for what is past."

"O say not soe, thou holy friar;
  I pray thee, say not soe:
For since my true-love dyed for mee,
  'Tis meet my teares should flow.

"And will he never come again?
  Will he ne'er come again?
Ah! no, he is dead, and laid in his grave,
  For ever to remain.

"His cheek was redder than the rose;
  The comeliest youth was he!
But he is dead and laid in his grave:
  Alas! and woe is me!"

"Sigh no more, lady, sigh no more,
  Men were deceivers ever:
One foot on sea and one on land,
  To one thing constant never.

"Hadst thou been fond, he had been false,
  And left thee sad and heavy:
For young men ever were fickle found,
  Since summer trees were leafy."

"Now say not soe, thou holy friar,
  I pray thee say not soe:
My love he had the truest heart:
  O, he was ever true!

"And art thou dead, thou much-lov'd youth,
  And didst thou dye for mee?
Then farewell home; for evermore
  A pilgrim I will bee.

"But first upon my true-love's grave
    My weary limbs I'll lay,
And thrice I'll kiss the green grass-turf
    That wraps his breathless clay."

" Yet stay, fair lady : rest awhile
   Beneath this cloyster wall :
See through the hawthorn blows the cold wind,
   And drizzly rain doth fall."

" O stay me not, thou holy friar ;
   O stay me not, I pray :
No drizzly rain that falls on me
   Can wash my fault away."

" Yet stay, fair lady, turn again,
   And dry those pearly tears ;
For see, beneath this gown of gray
   Thy owne true-love appears.

" Here, forced by grief and hopeless love,
   These holy weeds I sought ;
And here amid these lonely walls
   To end my days I thought.

" But haply, for my year of grace
   Is not yet pass'd away,
Might I still hope to win thy love,
   No longer would I stay."

" Now farewell grief, and welcome joy
   Once more unto my heart ;
For since I've found thee, lovely youth,
   We never more will part."

THE VICAR

SOME years ago, ere Time and Taste
   Had turn'd our parish topsy-turvy,
When Darnel Park was Darnel Waste,
   And roads as little known as scurvy,
The man who lost his way between
   St. Mary's Hill and Sandy Thicket,
Was always shown across the Green,
   And guided to the Parson's wicket.

Back flew the bolt of lissom lath :
   Fair Margaret, in her tidy kirtle,
Led the lorn traveller up the path,
   Through clean-clipt rows of box and myrtle :
And Don and Sancho, Tramp and Tray,
   Upon the parlour steps collected,
Wagg'd all their tails, and seem'd to say,
   "Our master knows you ; you're expected !"

Up rose the Reverend Dr. Brown,
　　Up rose the Doctor's " winsome marrow :"
The lady lay her knitting down,
　　Her husband clasp'd his ponderous Barrow :
Whate'er the stranger's caste or creed,
　　Pundit or papist, saint or sinner,
He found a stable for his steed,
　　And welcome for himself, and dinner.

If, when he reach'd his journey's end
  And warm'd himself in court or college,
He had not gain'd an honest friend,
  And twenty curious scraps of knowledge:
If he departed as he came,
  With no new light on love or liquor,
Good sooth, the traveller was to blame,
  And not the vicarage, or the Vicar.

His talk was like a stream which runs,
  With rapid change, from rock to roses:
It slipp'd from politics to puns,
  It pass'd from Mahomet to Moses;
Beginning with the laws which keep
  The planets in their radiant courses,
And ending with some precept deep,
  For dressing eels or shoeing horses.

He was a shrewd and sound divine,
  Of loud Dissent the mortal terror;
And when, by dint of page and line,
  He 'stablish'd truth, or started error,
The Baptist found him far too deep;
  The Deist sigh'd, with saving sorrow;
And the lean Levite went to sleep,
  And dream'd of tasting pork to-morrow.

His sermons never said or show'd
  That earth is foul, that heaven is gracious,
Without refreshment on the road
  From Jerome or from Athanasius:
And sure a righteous zeal inspired
  The hand and head that penn'd and plann'd them,
For all who understood, admired,
  And some who did not understand them.

THE VICAR.

He wrote, too, in a quiet way,
　　Small treatises, and smaller verses;
And sage remarks on chalk and clay,
　　And hints to noble lords and nurses;
True histories of last year's ghost,
　　Lines to a ringlet or a turban;
And trifles for the Morning Post,
　　And nothing for Sylvanus Urban.

He did not think all mischief fair,
　　Although he had a knack of joking;
He did not make himself a bear,
　　Although he had a taste for smoking;
And when religious sects ran mad,
　　He held, in spite of all his learning,
That if a man's belief is bad,
　　It will not be improved by burning.

And he was kind, and loved to sit
　　In the low hut or garnish'd cottage,
And praise the farmer's homely wit,
　　And share the widow's homelier pottage:
At his approach complaint grew mild,
　　And when his hand unbarr'd the shutter,
The clammy lips of Fever smiled
　　The welcome which they could not utter.

He always had a tale for me,
　　Of Julius Cæsar or of Venus;
From him I learn'd the Rule of Three,
　　Cat's-cradle, leap-frog, and Quæ genus.
I used to singe his powder'd wig,
　　To steal the staff he put such trust in;
And make the puppy dance a jig,
　　When he began to quote Augustin.

Alack the change! in vain I look
  For haunts in which my boyhood trifled,—
The level lawn, the trickling brook,
  The trees I climb'd, the beds I rifled:
The church is larger than before,
  You reach it by a carriage entry:
It holds three hundred people more,
  And pews are fitted up for gentry.

Sit in the Vicar's seat: you'll hear
  The doctrine of a gentle Johnian,
Whose hand is white, whose tone is clear,
  Whose style is very Ciceronian.
Where is the old man laid? Look down,
  And construe on the slab before you,
"HIC JACET GULIELMUS BROWN,
  VIR NULLA NON DONANDUS LAURO."

SUMMER WOODS.

Come ye into the summer woods,
  There entereth no annoy;
All greenly wave the chesnut leaves,
  And the earth is full of joy.

I cannot tell you half the sights
  Of beauty you may see
The bursts of golden sunshine,
  And many a shady tree.

There, lightly swung, in bowery glades,
  The honeysuckles twine;
There blooms the rose-red campion,
  And the dark-blue columbine.

There grows the four-leaved plant, "true-love,"
  In some dusk woodland spot;
There grows the enchanter's night-shade,
  And the wood forget-me-not.

And many a merry bird is there,
  Unscared by lawless men.
The blue-wing'd jay, the woodpecker,
  And the golden-crested wren.

Come down, and ye shall see them all,
  The timid and the bold;
For their sweet life of pleasantness,
  It is not to be told.

And far within that summer wood,
　　Among the leaves so green,
There flows a little gurgling brook,
　　The brightest e'er was seen.

There come the little gentle birds,
    Without a fear of ill:
Down to the murmuring water's edge,
    And freely drink their fill:

And dash about and splash about—
    The merry little things!
And look askance with bright black eyes,
    And flirt their dripping wings.

I've seen the freakish squirrels drop
    Down from their leafy tree,
The little squirrels with the old, -
    Great joy it was to me!

And down unto the running brook
    I've seen them nimbly go;
And the bright water seem'd to speak
    A welcome kind and low.

The nodding plants they bow'd their heads,
    As if, in heartsome cheer,
They spake unto those little things,
    " 'Tis merry living here!"

Oh, how my heart ran o'er with joy!
    I saw that all was good,
And how we might glean up delight
    All round us, if we would!

And many a wood-mouse dwelleth there,
    Beneath the old wood-shade,
And all day long has work to do,
    Nor is of aught afraid.

The green shoots grow above their heads,
  And roots so fresh and fine
Beneath their feet; nor is there strife
  'Mong them for *mine* and *thine*.

There is enough for every one,
  And they lovingly agree:
We might learn a lesson, all of us,
  Beneath the green-wood tree.

A WET SHEET AND A FLOWING SEA

A wet sheet and a flowing sea,
  A wind that follows fast,
And fills the white and rustling sail,
  And bends the gallant mast,
And bends the gallant mast, my boys,
  While, like the eagle free,
Away the good ship flies, and leaves
  Old England on the lee.

O, for a soft and gentle wind!
  I heard a fair one cry:
But give to me the swelling breeze,
  And white waves heaving high,
The white waves heaving high, my lads,
  The good ship tight and free,
The world of waters is our home,
  And merry men are we.

There's tempest in yon horned moon,
  And lightning in yon cloud :
And hark, the music, mariners !
  The wind is wakening loud
The wind is wakening loud, my boys.
  The lightning flashes free.
The hollow oak our palace is.
  Our heritage the sea.

THE SPANISH ARMADA.

Attend, all ye who list to hear our noble England's praise;
I tell of the thrice-famous deeds she wrought in ancient days,
When that great Fleet Invincible against her bore in vain
The richest spoils of Mexico, the stoutest hearts of Spain.
It was about the lovely close of a warm summer day.
There came a gallant merchant-ship full sail to Plymouth Bay;
Her crew hath seen Castile's black fleet, beyond Aurigny's isle,
At earliest twilight, on the waves lie heaving many a mile;
At sunrise she escaped their van, by God's especial grace;
And the tall Pinta, till the noon, had held her close in chase.
Forthwith a guard at every gun was placed along the wall;
The beacon blazed upon the roof of Edgecumbe's lofty hall;
Many a light fishing-bark put out to pry along the coast;
And with loose rein and bloody spur rode inland many a post
With his white hair unbonneted, the stout old sheriff comes
Behind him march the halberdiers, before him sound the drums;
His yeomen round the market-cross make clear an ample space,
For there behoves him to set up the standard of Her Grace.
And haughtily the trumpets peal, and gaily dance the bells,
As slow upon the labouring wind the royal blazon swells.
Look how the Lion of the sea lifts up his ancient crown,
And underneath his deadly paw treads the gay lilies down.
So stalk'd he when he turn'd to flight, on that famed Picard field,
Bohemia's plume, and Genoa's bow, and Cæsar's eagle shield;

So glared he when at Agincourt in wrath he turn'd to bay.
And crush'd and torn beneath his claws the princely hunters lay.
Ho! strike the flagstaff deep, Sir Knight: ho! scatter flowers, fair maids:
Ho! gunners, fire a loud salute; ho, gallants, draw your blades:
Thou sun, shine on her joyously,—ye breezes, waft her wide;
Our glorious SEMPER EADEM, the banner of our pride.

The freshening breeze of eve unfurl'd that banner's massy fold.
The parting gleam of sunshine kiss'd that haughty scroll of gold;
Night sunk upon the dusky beach, and on the purple sea,—
Such night in England ne'er had been, nor e'er again shall be.
From Eddystone to Berwick bounds, from Lynn to Milford Bay,
That time of slumber was as bright and busy as the day;
For swift to east and swift to west the ghastly war-flame spread,
High on St. Michael's Mount it shone: it shone on Beachy Head.
Far on the deep the Spaniard saw, along each southern shire,
Cape beyond cape, in endless range, those twinkling points of fire.
The fisher left his skiff to rock on Tamar's glittering waves:
The rugged miners pour'd to war from Mendip's sunless caves:
O'er Longleat's towers, o'er Cranbourne's oaks, the fiery herald flew:
He roused the shepherds of Stonehenge, the rangers of Beaulieu:
Right sharp and quick the bells all night rang out from Bristol town,
And ere the day three hundred horse had met on Clifton down;
The sentinel on Whitehall Gate look'd forth into the night,
And saw o'erhanging Richmond Hill the streak of blood-red light.
Then bugle's note and cannon's roar the death-like silence broke,
And with one start, and with one cry, the royal city woke.
At once on all her stately gates arose the answering fires:
At once the wild alarum clash'd from all her reeling spires:
From all the batteries of the Tower peal'd loud the voice of fear;
And all the thousand masts of Thames sent back a louder cheer:

And from the farthest wards was heard the rush of hurrying feet,
And the broad streams of flags and pikes dash'd down each roaring street;
And broader still became the blaze, and louder still the din,
As fast from every village round the horse came spurring in:

And eastward straight from wild Blackheath the warlike errand went,
And roused in many an ancient hall the gallant squires of Kent.
Southward from Surrey's pleasant hills flew those bright couriers forth;
High on bleak Hampstead's swarthy moor they started for the north;

And on, and on, without a pause, untired they bounded still,
All night from tower to tower they sprang; they sprang from hill to hill
Till the proud peak unfurl'd the flag o'er Darwin's rocky dales,
Till like volcanoes flared to heaven the stormy hills of Wales,
Till twelve fair counties saw the blaze on Malvern's lonely height,
Till stream'd in crimson on the wind the Wrekin's crest of light,
Till broad and fierce the star came forth on Ely's stately fane,
And tower and hamlet rose in arms o'er all the boundless plain;
Till Belvoir's lordly terraces the sign to Lincoln sent,
And Lincoln sped the message on o'er the wide vale of Trent;
Till Skiddaw saw the fire that burn'd on Gaunt's embattled pile,
And the red glare on Skiddaw roused the burghers of Carlisle.

DEAR IS MY LITTLE NATIVE VALE.

Dear is my little native vale,
 The ring-dove builds and murmurs there,
Close by my cot she tells her tale,
 To every passing villager.
The squirrel leaps from tree to tree,
And shells his nuts at liberty.

In orange-groves and myrtle bowers,
 That breathe a gale of fragrance round,
I charm the fairy-footed hours,
 With my loved lute's romantic sound;
Or crowns of living laurel weave,
For those that win the race at eve.

The shepherd's horn at break of day,
 The ballet danced in twilight glade,
The canzonet and roundelay,
 Sung in the silent green-wood shade:
These simple joys, that never fail,
Shall bind me to my native vale.

BONNIE JEAN.

THERE was a lass, and she was fair,
    At kirk and market to be seen;
When a' the fairest maids were met,
    The fairest maid was bonnie Jean.

And aye she wrought her mammie's wark,
    And aye she sang sae merrily:
The blythest bird upon the bush
    Had ne'er a lighter heart than she.

But hawks will rob the tender joys
    That bless the little lintwhite's nest;
And frost will blight the fairest flowers,
    And love will break the soundest rest.

Young Robie was the brawest lad,
    The flower and pride of a' the glen;
And he had owsen, sheep, and kye,
    And wanton naigies nine or ten.

He gaed wi' Jeanie to the tryste,
    He danced wi' Jeanie on the down;
And lang ere witless Jeanie wist,
    Her heart was tint, her peace was stown.

As in the bosom o' the stream
    The moon-beam dwells at dewy e'en;
So trembling, pure, was tender love,
    Within the breast o' bonnie Jean.

And now she works her mammie's wark,
    And aye she sighs wi' care and pain;
Yet wistna what her ail might be,
    Or what wad mak' her weel again.

But didna Jeanie's heart loup light,
    And didna joy blink in her ee,
As Robie tauld a tale o' love,
    Ae e'enin on the lily lea?

The sun was sinking in the west,
    The birds sang sweet in ilka grove,
His cheek to hers he fondly prest,
    And whisper'd thus his tale o' love:

"O Jeanie fair, I lo'e thee dear;
    O canst thou think to fancy me?
Or wilt thou leave thy mammie's cot,
    And learn to tent the farms wi' me?

"At barn or byre thou shalt na drudge,
    Or naething else to trouble thee;
But stray amang the heather-bells,
    And tent the waving corn wi' me."

Now what could artless Jeanie do?
    She had nae will to say him na:
At length she blush'd a sweet consent,
    And love was aye between them twa.

THE VILLAGE BLACKSMITH.

Under a spreading chestnut tree
   The village smithy stands:
The smith, a mighty man is he,
   With large and sinewy hands,
And the muscles of his brawny arms
   Are strong as iron bands.

His hair is crisp, and black, and long,
   His face is like the tan;
His brow is wet with honest sweat,
   He earns whate'er he can,
And looks the whole world in the face,
   For he owes not any man.

Week in, week out, from morn till night,
   You can hear his bellows blow;
You can hear him swing his heavy sledge,
   With measured beat and slow,
Like a sexton ringing the village bell,
   When the evening sun is low.

And children coming home from school
  Look in at the open door;
They love to see the flaming forge,
  And hear the bellows roar,
And catch the burning sparks that fly
  Like chaff from a threshing-floor.

He goes on Sunday to the church,
   And sits among his boys;
He hears the parson pray and preach,
   He hears his daughter's voice
Singing in the village choir,
   And it makes his heart rejoice.

It sounds to him like her mother's voice
   Singing in Paradise!
He needs must think of her once more,
   How in the grave she lies;
And with his hard rough hand he wipes
   A tear out of his eyes.

Toiling, rejoicing, sorrowing,
   Onward through life he goes;
Each morning sees some task begin,
   Each evening sees its close;
Something attempted, something done,
   Has earn'd a night's repose.

Thanks, thanks to thee, my worthy friend,
   For the lesson thou hast taught!
Thus at the flaming forge of life
   Our fortunes must be wrought;
Thus on its sounding anvil shaped
   Each burning deed and thought.

THE WISH.

MINE be a cot beside the hill;
   A bee-hive's hum shall soothe my ear;
A willow brook, that turns a mill,
   With many a fall, shall linger near.

The swallow, oft, beneath my thatch,
   Shall twitter from her clay-built nest;
Oft shall the pilgrim lift the latch,
   And share my meal, a welcome guest.

Around my ivy'd porch shall spring
   Each fragrant flower that drinks the dew;
And Lucy, at her wheel, shall sing,
   In russet gown and apron blue.

The village church, among the trees,
   Where first our marriage vows were given,
With merry peals shall swell the breeze,
   And point with taper spire to heaven.

A GLEAM OF SUNSHINE.

This is the place. Stand still, my steed;
  Let me review the scene,
And summon from the shadowy Past
  The forms that once have been.

The Past and Present here unite
  Beneath Time's flowing tide,
Like footprints hidden by a brook,
  But seen on either side.

Here runs the highway to the town;
   There the green lane descends,
Through which I walk'd to church with thee,
   O gentlest of my friends!

The shadow of the linden-trees
   Lay moving on the grass;
Between them and the moving boughs,
   A shadow, thou didst pass.

Thy dress was like the lilies,
   And thy heart as pure as they:
One of God's holy messengers
   Did walk with me that day.

I saw the branches of the trees
   Bend down thy touch to meet,
The clover-blossoms in the grass
   Rise up to kiss thy feet.

"Sleep, sleep to-day, tormenting cares,
   Of earth and folly born!"
Solemnly sang the village choir,
   On that sweet Sabbath morn.

Through the closed blinds the golden sun
   Pour'd in a dusty beam,
Like the celestial ladder seen
   By Jacob in his dream.

And ever and anon, the wind,
   Sweet-scented with the hay,
Turn'd o'er the hymn-book's fluttering leaves,
   That on the window lay.

Long was the good man's sermon,
　Yet it seem'd not so to me;
For he spake of Ruth the beautiful,
　And still I thought of thee.

Long was the prayer he utter'd,
　Yet it seem'd not so to me;
For in my heart I pray'd with him,
　And still I thought of thee.

But now, alas! the place seems changed;
　Thou art no longer here;
Part of the sunshine of the scene
　With thee did disappear.

Though thoughts, deep-rooted in my heart,
　Like pine-trees dark and high,
Subdue the light of noon, and breathe
　A low and ceaseless sigh;

This memory brightens o'er the past,
　As when the sun, conceal'd
Behind some cloud that near us hangs,
　Shines on a distant field.

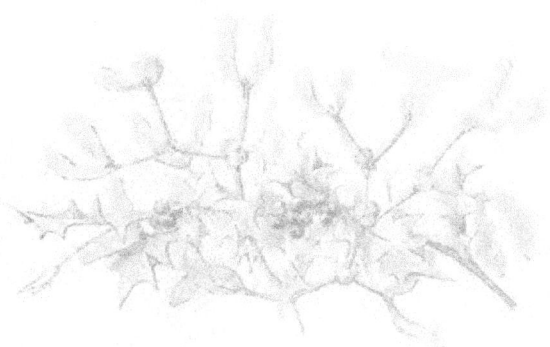

ROBIN REDBREAST.

GOOD-BYE, good-bye to Summer!
  For Summer's nearly done;
The garden smiling faintly,
  Cool breezes in the sun:
Our thrushes now are silent,
  Our swallows flown away,—
But Robin's here, in coat of brown,
  And scarlet breast-knot gay.
Robin, Robin Redbreast,
  O Robin dear!
Robin sings so sweetly
  In the falling of the year.

Bright yellow, red, and orange,
  The leaves come down in hosts;
The trees are Indian Princes,
  But soon they'll turn to ghosts;
The leathery pears and apples
  Hang russet on the bough;
It's Autumn, Autumn, Autumn late,
  'Twill soon be Winter now.

Robin, Robin Redbreast,
    O Robin dear!
And what will this poor Robin do?
    For pinching days are near.

The fireside for the cricket,
  The wheat-stack for the mouse,
When trembling night-winds whistle
  And moan all round the house;
The frosty ways like iron,
  The branches plumed with snow.
Alas! in Winter dead and dark,
  Where can poor Robin go?
Robin, Robin Redbreast,
  O Robin dear!
And a crumb of bread for Robin,
  His little heart to cheer.

A WALK IN A CHURCHYARD.

We walk'd within the churchyard bounds,
  My little boy and I,
He laughing, running happy rounds,
  I pacing mournfully.

"Nay, child! it is not well," I said,
  "Among the graves to shout,
To laugh and play among the dead,
  And make this noisy rout."

A moment to my side he clung,
  Leaving his merry play,
A moment still'd his joyous tongue,
  Almost as hush'd as they:

Then, quite forgetting the command,
  In life's exulting burst
Of early glee, let go my hand,
  Joyous as at the first.

And now I did not check him more,
  For, taught by Nature's face,
I had grown wiser than before,
  Ev'n in that moment's space:

She spread no funeral pall above
  That patch of churchyard ground;
But the same azure vault of love
  As hung o'er all around,

And white clouds o'er that spot would pass
  As freely as elsewhere;
The sunshine on no other grass
  A richer hue might wear.

And form'd from out that very mould
  In which the dead did lie.
The daisy, with its eye of gold,
  Look'd up into the sky.

The rook was wheeling over head,
  Nor hasten'd to be gone;
The small bird did its glad notes shed,
  Perch'd on a gray head-stone.

And God, I said, would never give
  This light upon the earth,
Nor bid in Childhood's heart to live
  These springs of gushing mirth,

If our one wisdom were to mourn,
  And linger with the dead,
To nurse, as wisest, thoughts forlorn
  Of worm and early bed.

Oh, no! the glory earth puts on,
  The child's uncheck'd delight,
Both witness to a triumph won
  (If we but judged aright);

A triumph won o'er Sin and Death—
  From these the Saviour saves;
And, like a happy infant, Faith
  Can play among the graves!

THE SOLDIER'S DREAM.

Our bugles sang truce—for the night-cloud had lower'd,
  And the sentinel stars set their watch in the sky;
And thousands had sunk on the ground overpower'd,
  The weary to sleep, and the wounded to die.

When reposing that night on my pallet of straw,
　By the wolf-scaring faggot that guarded the slain,
At the dead of the night a sweet vision I saw,
　And thrice ere the morning I dreamt it again.

Methought from the battle-field's dreadful array,
　Far, far I had roam'd on a desolate track:
'Twas Autumn, — and sunshine arose on the way
　To the home of my fathers, that welcomed me back.

I flew to the pleasant fields, traversed so oft
　In life's morning march, when my bosom was young;
I heard my own mountain-goats bleating aloft,
　And knew the sweet strain that the corn-reapers sung.

Then pledged we the wine-cup, and fondly I swore
　From my home and my weeping friends never to part;
My little ones kiss'd me a thousand times o'er,
　And my wife sobb'd aloud in her fulness of heart.

"Stay, stay with us,—rest! thou art weary and worn!"
　And fain was their war-broken soldier to stay;
But sorrow return'd with the dawning of morn,
　And the voice in my dreaming ear melted away.

THE LOVELY LASS OF INVERNESS.

There lived a lass in Inverness,
   She was the pride of a' the town,
Blythe as the lark on gowan-tap,
   When frae the nest but newly flown.
At kirk she won the auld folks' luve,
   At dance she wan the young men's een;
She was the blythest ay o' the blythe,
   At wooster-trystes or Halloween.

As I came in by Inverness,
   The simmer sun was sinking down,
O there I saw the weel-faur'd lass,
   And she was greeting through the town.
The grey-hair'd men were a' i' the streets,
   And auld dames crying (sad to see!)
" The flower o' the lads of Inverness
   Lie dead upon Culloden-lee!"

She tore her haffet-links of gowd,
   And dighted ay her comely ee;
" My father's head's on Carlisle wall,
   At Preston sleep my brethren three!
I thought my heart could hand nae mair,
   Mae tears could ever blin' my ee;
But the fa' o' ane has burst my heart—
   A dearer ane there couldna be!

' He trysted me o' love yestreen,
    Of love-tokens he gave me three;
But he's faulded i' the arms o' weir,
    O ne'er again to think o' me!
The forest flowers shall be my bed,
    My food shall be the wild berrie;
The fa' o' the leaf shall co'er me cauld,
    And wauken'd again I winna be!"

O weep, O weep, ye Scottish dames,
    Weep till ye blin' a mither's ee;
Nae reeking ha' in fifty miles,
    But naked corses sad to see!
O spring is blythesome to the year,
    Trees sprout, flowers spring, and birds sing hie;
But oh! what spring can raise them up,
    That lie on dread Culloden-lee?

The hand o' God hung heavy here,
    And lightly touch'd foul tyrannie;
It struck the righteous to the ground,
    And lifted the destroyer hie.
"But there's a day," quo' my God in prayer,
    "When righteousness shall bear the gree;
I'll rake the wicked low i' the dust,
    And wauken, in bliss, the gude man's ee!"

THE OLD GREEN LANE.

'Twas the very merry summer time,
  That garlands hills and dales,
And the south wind rung a fairy chime
  Upon the foxglove bells;

The cuckoo stood on the lady-birch,
　　To bid her last good-bye —
The lark sprung over the village church,
　　And whistled to the sky;
And we had come from the harvest sheaves,
　　A blythe and tawny train,
And track'd our paths with poppy leaves
　　Along the old green lane.

'Twas a pleasant way on a sunny day,
　　And we were a happy set,
And we idly bent where the streamlet went,
　　To get our fingers wet;
With the dog-rose there, and the orchis there,
　　And the woodbine twining through,
With the broad trees meeting everywhere,
　　And the grass still dank with dew.
Ah! we all forgot, in that blissful spot,
　　The names of care and pain,
As we lay on the bank, by the shepherd's cot,
　　To rest in the old green lane.

Oh, days gone by! I can but sigh
　　As I think on that rich hour,
When my heart in its glee but seem'd to be
　　Another wood-side flower;
For though the trees be still as fair,
　　And the wild bloom still as gay—
Though the south wind sends as sweet an air,
　　And heaven as bright a day!—
Yet the merry set are far and wide,
　　And we ne'er shall meet again,
We shall never ramble side by side
　　Along that green old lane.

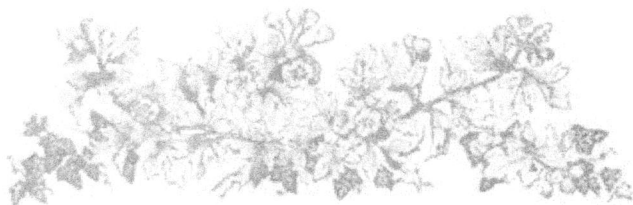

THE MAY QUEEN.

You must wake and call me early, call me early, mother dear;
To-morrow 'ill be the happiest time of all the glad New-year;
Of all the glad New-year, mother, the maddest merriest day;
For I'm to be Queen o' the May, mother, I'm to be Queen o' the May.

There's many a black black eye, they say, but none so bright as mine;
There's Margaret and Mary, there's Kate and Caroline;
But none so fair as little Alice in all the land, they say,
So I'm to be Queen o' the May, mother, I'm to be Queen o' the May.

I sleep so sound all night, mother, that I shall never wake,
If you do not call me loud when the day begins to break;
But I must gather knots of flowers, and buds and garlands gay,
For I'm to be Queen o' the May, mother, I'm to be Queen o' the May.

As I came up the valley, whom think ye should I see,
But Robin leaning on the bridge beneath the hazel-tree?
He thought of that sharp look, mother, I gave him yesterday,
But I'm to be Queen o' the May, mother, I'm to be Queen o' the May.

He thought I was a ghost, mother, for I was all in white,
And I ran by him without speaking, like a flash of light.
They call me cruel-hearted, but I care not what they say,
For I'm to be Queen o' the May, mother, I'm to be Queen o' the May.

They say he's dying all for love, but that can never be:
They say his heart is breaking, mother — what is that to me?
There's many a bolder lad 'll woo me any summer day,
For I'm to be Queen o' the May, mother, I'm to be Queen o' the May.

Little Ellie shall go with me to-morrow to the green,
And you 'll be there, too, mother, to see me made the Queen ;
For the shepherd lads on every side 'ill come from far away,
And I 'm to be Queen o' the May, mother, I 'm to be Queen o' the May.

The honeysuckle round the porch has wov'n its wavy bowers,
And by the meadow-trenches blow the faint sweet cuckoo-flowers ;
And the wild marsh-marigold shines like fire in swamps and hollows gray,
And I 'm to be Queen o' the May, mother, I 'm to be Queen o' the May.

The night-winds come and go, mother, upon the meadow-grass,
And the happy stars above them seem to brighten as they pass ;
There will not be a drop of rain the whole of the livelong day,
And I 'm to be Queen o' the May, mother, I 'm to be Queen o' the May.

All the valley, mother, 'ill be fresh and green and still,
And the cowslip and the crowfoot are over all the hill,
And the rivulet in the flowery dale 'ill merrily glance and play,
For I 'm to be Queen o' the May, mother, I 'm to be Queen o' the May.

So you must wake and call me early, call me early, mother dear,
To-morrow 'ill be the happiest time of all the glad New-year ;
To-morrow 'ill be of all the year the maddest merriest day,
For I 'm to be Queen o' the May, mother, I 'm to be Queen o' the May.

AULD ROBIN GRAY.

When the sheep are in the fauld, when the cows come hame,
When a' the weary world to quiet rest are gane,
The woes of my heart fa' in showers frae my ee,
Unkenn'd by my gudeman, who soundly sleeps by me.

Young Jamie loo'd me well, and sought me for his bride,
But saving ae crown-piece, he'd naething else beside.
To make the crown a pound my Jamie gaed to sea;
And the crown and the pound, oh! they were baith for me!

Before he had been gane a twelvemonth and a day,
My father brak his arm, our cow was stown away;
My mother she fell sick—my Jamie was at sea—
And auld Robin Gray—oh! he came a-courting me!

My father couldna work, my mother couldna spin;
I toil'd day and night, but their bread I couldna win;
Auld Rob maintain'd them baith, and, wi' tears in his ee,
Said, "Jenny, oh! for their sakes, will you marry me?"

My heart it said na, and I look'd for Jamie back;
But hard blew the winds, and his ship was a wrack:
His ship it was a wrack! why didna Jamie dee?
Or wherefore am I spared to cry out, Woe is me!

My father argued sair – my mother didna speak,
But she look'd in my face till my heart was like to break:
They gied him my hand, but my heart was in the sea:
And so auld Robin Gray, he was gudeman to me.

I hadna been his wife a week but only four,
When, mournfu' as I sat on the stane at my door,
I saw my Jamie's ghaist   I couldna think it he,
Till he said, " I'm come hame, my love, to marry thee!"

Oh! sair, sair did we greet, and mickle say of a';
Ae kiss we took   nae mair; I bad him gang awa'.
I wish that I were dead, but I'm no like to dee:
For oh! I am but young to cry out, Woe is me!

I gang like a ghaist, and I carena much to spin;
I darena think o' Jamie, for that wad be a sin:
But I will do my best a gude wife aye to be,
For auld Robin Gray, oh! he is sae kind to me.

THE OPEN WINDOW.

The old house by the lindens
  Stood silent in the shade,
And on the gravell'd pathway
  The light and shadow play'd.

I saw the nursery windows
  Wide open to the air;
But the faces of the children,
  They were no longer there.

The large Newfoundland house-dog
  Was standing by the door;
He look'd for his little playmates,
  Who would return no more.

They walk'd not under the lindens,
  They play'd not in the hall;
But shadow, and silence, and sadness,
  Were hanging over all.

The birds sang in the branches,
   With sweet, familiar tone;
But the voices of the children
   Will be heard in dreams alone!

And the boy that walk'd beside me,
   He could not understand
Why closer in mine, ah! closer,
   I press'd his warm, soft hand!

RUPERT'S MARCH.

Carabine slung, stirrup well hung,
Flagon at saddle-bow merrily swung;
Toss up the ale, for our flag, like a sail,
Struggles and swells in the hot July gale.
Colours fling out, and then give them a shout—
We are the gallants to put them to rout.

Flash all your swords, like Tartarian hordes,
And scare the prim ladies of Puritan lords;
Our steel caps shall blaze through the long summer days,
As we, galloping, sing our mad Cavalier lays.
Then banners advance!   By the lilies of France,
We are the gallants to lead them a dance!

Ring the bells back, though the sexton look black,
Defiance to knaves who are hot on our track.
"Murder and fire!" shout louder and higher;
Remember Edge-hill and the red-dabbled mire,
When our steeds we shall stall in the Parliament hall,
And shake the old nest till the roof-tree shall fall.

Froth it up, girl, till it splash every curl,
October's the liquor for trooper and earl;
Bubble it up, merry gold in the cup,
We never may taste of to-morrow night's sup.
(Those red ribbons glow on thy bosom below
Like apple-tree bloom on a hillock of snow.)

1 7

No, by my word, there never shook sword
Better than this in the clutch of a lord;
The blue streaks that run are as bright in the sun
As the veins on the brow of that loveliest one;
No deep light of the sky, when the twilight is nigh,
Glitters more bright than this blade to the eye.

    *   *   *   *   *   *

Well, whatever may hap, this rusty steel-cap
Will keep out full many a pestilent rap;
This buff, though it's old and not laced with gold,
Will guard me from rapier as well as from cold;
This scarf, rent and torn, though its colour is worn,
Shone gay as a page's but yesterday morn.

Here is a dint from the jagg of a flint,
Thrown by a Puritan, just as a hint;
But this stab through the buff was a warning more rough,
When Coventry city arose in a huff;
And I met with this gash, as we rode with a crash
Into Noll's pikes on the banks of the Ash.

No jockey or groom wears so draggled a plume
As this that's just drench'd in the swift-flowing Froom.
Red grew the tide ere we reach'd the steep side,
And steaming the hair of old Barbary's hide;
But for branch of that oak that saved me a stroke,
I had sunk there like herring in pickle to soak.

Pistolet crack flash'd bright on our track,
And even the foam of the water turn'd black.
They were twenty to one, our poor rapier to gun,
But we charged up the bank, and we lost only one;
So I saved the old flag, though it was but a rag,
And the sword in my hand was snapp'd off to a jagg.

The water was churn'd as we wheel'd and we turn'd,
And the dry brake to scare out the vermin we burn'd.
We gave our halloo, and our trumpet we blew ;
Of all their stout fifty we left them but two ;
With a mock and a laugh, won their banner and staff,
And trod down the cornets as thrashers do chaff.

Saddle my roan, his back is a throne,
Better than velvet or gold, you will own,
Look to your match, or some harm you may catch,
For treason has always some mischief to hatch :
And Oliver's out with all Haslerigg's rout,
So I'm told by this shivering, white-liver'd scout.

We came over the downs, through village and towns,
In spite of the sneers, and the curses and frowns ;
Drowning their psalms, and stilling their qua'ms,
With a clatter and rattle of scabbards and arms,
Down the long street, with a trample of feet,
For the echo of hoofs to a Cavalier's sweet.

See black on each roof, at the sound of our hoof,
The Puritans gather, but keep them aloof ;
Their muskets are long, and they aim at a throng,
But woe to the weak when they challenge the strong !
Butt-end to the door, one hammer more,
Our pike-men rush in, and the struggle is o'er.

Storm through the gate, batter the plate,
Cram the red crucible into the grate :
Saddle-bags fill, Bob, Jenkin, and Will,
And spice the staved wine that runs out like a rill.
That maiden shall ride all to-day by my side,
Those ribbons are fitting a Cavalier's bride.

Does Baxter say right, that a bodice laced tight,
Should never be seen by the sun or the light?
Like stars from a wood, shine under that hood,
Eyes that are sparkling, though pious and good.
Surely this waist was by Providence placed,
By a true lover's arm to be often embraced.

Down on your knees, you villains in frieze,
A draught to King Charles, or a swing from those trees ;
Blow off this stiff lock, for 'tis useless to knock,
The ladies will pardon the noise and the shock,
From this bright dewy cheek, might I venture to speak,
I could kiss off the tears though she wept for a week.

Now loop me this scarf round the broken pike-staff,
'Twill do for a flag, though the Crop Heads may laugh.
Who was it blew ?   Give an halloo,
And hang out the pennon of crimson and blue ;
A volley of shot is a welcoming hot ;—
It cannot be troop of the murdering Scot ?

Fire the old mill on the brow of the hill,
Break down the plank that runs over the rill,
Bar the town gate ; if the burghers debate,
Shoot some to death, for the villains must wait ;
Rip up the lead from the roofing o'er head,
And melt it for bullets, or we shall be sped.

Now look to your buff, for steel is the stuff
To slash your brown jerkins with crimson enough ;
There burst a flash—I heard their drums crash ;
To horse ! now for race over moorland and plash ;
Ere the stars glimmer out, we will wake with a shout
The true men of York, who will welcome our rout.

We'll shake their red roofs with our echoing hoofs,
And flutter the dust from their tapestry woofs ;
Their old Minster shall ring with our " God save the King,"
And our horses shall drink at St. Christopher's spring ;
We shall welcome the meat, O the wine will taste sweet,
When our boots we fling off, and as brothers we meet.

THE MINUTE GUN.

WHEN in the storm on Albion's coast
The night-watch guards his wary post,
    From thoughts of danger free,
He marks some vessel's dusky form,
And hears, amid the howling storm,
    The minute gun at sea.

Swift on the shore a hardy few
The life-boat man with gallant crew,
    And dare the dangerous wave:
Through the wild surf they cleave their way,
Lost in the form, nor know dismay,
    For they go the crew to save.

But, oh! what rapture fills each breast
Of the hopeless crew of the ship distress'd!
Then, landed safe, what joy to tell
Of all the dangers that befell!
Then heard is no more,
By the watch on shore,
    The minute gun at sea.

THE IRISH EMIGRANT.

I'm sitting on the stile, Mary,
    Where we sat side by side,
On a bright May morning long ago,
    When first you were my bride.
The corn was springing fresh and green,
    And the lark sang loud and high,
And the red was on your lip, Mary,
    And the love light in your eye.

The place is little changed, Mary,
  The day's as bright as then ;
The lark's loud song is in my ear,
  And the corn is green again.
But I miss the clasp of your hand,
  And your warm breath on my cheek.
And I still keep listening for the words
  You never more may speak.

'Tis but a step down yonder lane,
  The village church stands near—
The church where we were wed, Mary,
  I see the spire from here.
But the grave-yard lies between, Mary,
  And my step might break your rest,
Where I've laid you, darling, down to sleep,
  With your baby on your breast.

I'm very lonely, now, Mary,
  For the poor make no new friends ;
But, oh! they love the better
  The few our Father sends.
And you were all I had, Mary,
  My blessing and my pride :
There's nothing left to care for now,
  Since my poor Mary died.

I'm bidding you a long farewell,
  My Mary kind and true.
But I'll not forget you, darling,
  In the land I'm going to.
They say there's bread and work for all,
  And the sun shines always there,
But I'll not forget old Ireland,
  Were it fifty times less fair.

AFTON WATER.

Flow gently, sweet Afton, among thy green braes,
Flow gently, I'll sing thee a song in thy praise;
My Mary's asleep by thy murmuring stream,
Flow gently, sweet Afton, disturb not her dream.

Thou stock-dove, whose echo resounds through the glen,
Ye wild whistling blackbirds in yon thorny den,
Thou green-crested lapwing, thy screaming forbear,
I charge you, disturb not my slumbering fair.

How lofty, sweet Afton, thy neighbouring hills,
Far mark'd with the courses of clear, winding rills;
There daily I wander as noon rises high,
My flocks and my Mary's sweet cot in my eye.

How pleasant thy banks and green valleys below,
Where wild in the woodlands the primroses blow:
There oft, as mild evening weeps over the lea,
The sweet-scented birk shades my Mary and me.

Thy crystal stream, Afton, how lovely it glides,
And winds by the cot where my Mary resides;
How wanton thy waters her snowy feet lave,
As gathering sweet flow'rets she stems thy clear wave.

Flow gently, sweet Afton, among thy green braes,
Flow gently, sweet river, the theme of my lays:
My Mary's asleep by thy murmuring stream,
Flow gently, sweet Afton, disturb not her dream.

THE INCHCAPE ROCK.

No stir in the air, no stir in the sea,
The ship was still as she could be;
Her sails from heaven received no motion,
Her keel was steady in the ocean.

Without either sign or sound of their shock,
The waves flow'd over the Inchcape Rock;
So little they rose, so little they fell,
They did not move the Inchcape Bell.

The Abbot of Aberbrothok
Had placed that bell on the Inchcape Rock;
On a buoy in the storm it floated and swung,
And over the waves its warning rung.

When the Rock was hid by the surge's swell,
The mariners heard the warning Bell;
And then they knew the perilous Rock,
And bless'd the Abbot of Aberbrothok.

The sun in heaven was shining gay,
All things were joyful on that day;
The sea-birds scream'd as they wheel'd round,
And there was joyaunce in their sound.

The buoy of the Inchcape Bell was seen,
A darker speck on the ocean green;
Sir Ralph the Rover walk'd his deck,
And he fix'd his eye on the darker speck.

He felt the cheering power of Spring,
It made him whistle, it made him sing;
His heart was mirthful to excess,
But the Rover's mirth was wickedness.

His eye was on the Inchcape float;
Quoth he, "My men, put out the boat,
And row me to the Inchcape Rock,
And I'll plague the Abbot of Aberbrothok."

116

THE INCHCAPE ROCK.

The boat is lower'd, the boatmen row,
And to the Inchcape Rock they go;
Sir Ralph bent over from the boat,
And he cut the Bell from the Inchcape float.

Down sunk the Bell with a gurgling sound,
The bubbles rose and burst around;
Quoth Sir Ralph. "The next who comes to the Rock
Won't bless the Abbot of Aberbrothok."

Sir Ralph the Rover sail'd away,
He scour'd the seas for many a day;
And now, grown rich with plunder'd store,
He steers his course for Scotland's shore.

So thick a haze o'erspreads the sky,
They cannot see the sun on high;
The wind hath blown a gale all day,
At evening it hath died away.

On the deck the Rover takes his stand;
So dark it is, they see no land.
Quoth Sir Ralph. "It will be lighter soon,
For there is the dawn of the rising moon."

"Canst hear," said one, "the breakers roar?
For methinks we should be near the shore."
"Now where we are I cannot tell.
But I wish I could hear the Inchcape Bell."

They hear no sound, the swell is strong;
Though the wind hath fallen, they drift along.
Till the vessel strikes, with a shivering shock,
"O Christ! it is the Inchcape Rock!"

Sir Ralph the Rover tore his hair:
He cursed himself in his despair:
The waves rush in on every side,
The ship is sinking beneath the tide.

But even in his dying fear
One dreadful sound could the Rover hear,—
A sound as if, with the Inchcape Bell,
The Devil below was ringing his knell.

THE MILLER OF THE DEE.

There dwelt a miller hale and bold,
   Beside the river Dee;
He work'd and sang from morn to night,
   No lark more blythe than he;
And this the burden of his song
   For ever used to be,—
"I envy nobody: no, not I,
   And nobody envies me!"

"Thou 'rt wrong, my friend!" said old King Hal,
   "Thou 'rt wrong as wrong can be;
For could my heart be light as thine,
   I 'd gladly change with thee.
And tell me now what makes thee sing
   With voice so loud and free,
While I am sad, though I 'm the King,
   Beside the river Dee?"

The miller smiled and doff'd his cap:
   "I earn my bread," quoth he;
"I love my wife, I love my friend,
   I love my children three;
I owe no penny I cannot pay;—
   I thank the river Dee,
That turns the mill that grinds the corn,
   To feed my babes and me."

"Good friend!" said Hal, and sigh'd the while,
   "Farewell! and happy be:
But say no more, if thou'dst be true,
   That no one envies thee.
Thy mealy cap is worth my crown,—
   Thy mill my kingdom's fee!
Such men as thou are England's boast,
   O miller of the Dee!"

THE ARAB'S FAREWELL TO HIS STEED.

My beautiful! my beautiful! that standest meekly by,
With thy proudly arch'd and glossy neck, thy dark and fiery eye—
Fret not to roam the desert now with all thy winged speed,
I may not mount on thee again—thou 'rt sold, my Arab steed!
Fret not with that impatient hoof, snuff not the breezy wind,
The farther that thou fliest now, so far am I behind.
The stranger hath thy bridle-rein, thy master hath his gold,
Fleet limb'd and beautiful, farewell! thou 'rt sold, my steed, thou 'rt sold!

Farewell! those free untired limbs full many a mile must roam,
To reach the chill and wintry sky which clouds the stranger's home;
Some other hand, less fond, must now thy corn and bread prepare,
Thy silky mane, I braided once, must be another's care.
The morning sun shall dawn again, but never more with thee
Shall I gallop through the desert paths where we were wont to be.
Evening shall darken on the earth, and o'er the sandy plain
Some other steed, with slower step, shall bear me home again.

Yes! thou must go! the wild free breeze, the brilliant sun and sky,
Thy master's house,—from all of these my exiled one must fly.
Thy proud dark eye will grow less proud, thy step become less fleet,
And vainly shalt thou arch thy neck thy master's hand to meet.
Only in sleep shall I behold that dark eye glancing bright;
Only in sleep shall hear again that step so firm and light;
And when I raise my dreaming arm to check or cheer thy speed,
Then must I, starting, wake to feel thou 'rt sold, my Arab steed!

Ah! rudely then, unseen by me, some cruel hand may chide,
Till foam-wreaths lie, like crested waves, along thy panting side;
And the rich blood that 's in thee swells in thy indignant pain,
Till careless eyes which rest on thee, may count each starting vein.
Will they ill-use thee?   If I thought—but no, it cannot be—
Thou art so swift, yet easy curb'd—so gentle, yet so free.
And yet, if haply when thou 'rt gone, my lonely heart should yearn,
Can the same hand which casts thee off command thee to return?

Return?   Alas, my Arab steed! what shall thy master do,
When thou, who wert his all of joy, hast vanish'd from his view?
When the dim distance cheats mine eye, and, through the gathering tears.
Thy bright form for a moment like the false mirage appears.
Slow and unmounted will I roam with weary foot alone,
Where with fleet step and joyous bound thou oft hast borne me on:
And sitting down by that green well, will pause and sadly think,
'Twas here he bow'd his glossy neck, when last I saw him drink.

When last I saw him drink!   Away! the fever'd dream is o'er;
I could not live a day, and know that we should meet no more.
They tempted me, my beautiful! for hunger's power is strong;
They tempted me, my beautiful! but I have loved too long;

Who said that I had given thee up?   Who said that thou wert sold?
'Tis false, 'tis false! my Arab steed!   I fling them back their gold.
Thus, thus, I leap upon thy back, and scour the distant plains,—
Away!   who overtakes us now shall claim thee for his pains!

THE WELL OF ST. KEYNE.

A well there is in the west country,
   And a clearer one never was seen;
There is not a wife in the west country
   But has heard of the Well of St. Keyne.

An oak and an elm-tree stand beside,
   And behind doth an ash-tree grow,
And a willow from the bank above
   Droops to the water below.

A traveller came to the Well of St. Keyne;
   Joyfully he drew nigh,
For from cock-crow he had been travelling,
   And there was not a cloud in the sky.

He drank of the water so cool and clear,
   For thirsty and hot was he,
And he sat down upon the bank
   Under the willow-tree.

There came a man from the house hard by,
   At the Well to fill his pail;
On the well-side he rested it,
   And he bade the stranger hail.

"Now art thou a bachelor, stranger?" quoth he,
  "For an if thou hast a wife,
The happiest draught thou hast drank this day
    That ever thou didst in thy life.

"Or has thy good woman, if one thou hast,
    Ever here in Cornwall been?
For an if she have, I'll venture my life
    She has drank of the Well of St. Keyne."

"I have left a good woman who never was here,"
    The stranger he made reply,
"But that my draught should be the better for that,
    I pray you answer me why?"

"St. Keyne," quoth the Cornish-man, "many a time
    Drank of this crystal Well,
And before the Angel summon'd her,
    She laid on the water a spell.

"If the husband of this gifted Well
    Shall drink before his wife,
A happy man thenceforth is he,
    For he shall be master for life.

"But if the wife should drink of it first,—
    God help the husband then!"
The stranger stoop'd to the Well of St. Keyne,
    And drank of the water again.

"You drank of the Well I warrant betimes?"
    He to the Cornish-man said:
But the Cornish-man smiled as the Stranger spake,
    And sheepishly shook his head.

"I hasten'd as soon as the wedding was done,
    And left my wife in the porch :
But i' faith she had been wiser than me,
    For she took a bottle to church."

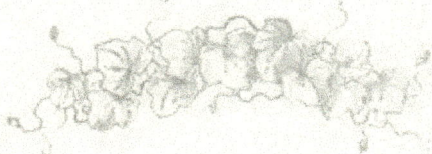

NIGHT.

Night is the time for rest ;
   How sweet, when labours close,
To gather round an aching breast
   The curtain of repose,
Stretch the tired limbs, and lay the head
Down on our own delightful bed!

Night is the time for dreams ;
   The gay romance of life,
When truth that is, and truth that seems,
   Mix in fantastic strife :
Ah ! visions, less beguiling far
Than waking dreams by daylight are !

Night is the time for toil ;
   To plough the classic field,
Intent to find the buried spoil
   Its wealthy furrows yield ;
Till all is ours that sages taught,
That poets sang and heroes wrought.

Night is the time to weep ;
   To wet with unseen tears
Those graves of memory where sleep
   The joys of other years ;
Hopes, that were angels at their birth,
But died when young, like things of earth.

Night is the time to watch:
  O'er ocean's dark expanse
To hail the Pleiades, or catch
  The full moon's earliest glance,
That brings into the home-sick mind
All we have loved and left behind.

Night is the time for care,
  Brooding on hours mis-spent,
To see the spectre of Despair
  Come to our lonely tent;
Like Brutus, 'midst his slumbering host,
Summon'd to die by Cæsar's ghost.

Night is the time to think;
  When, from the eye, the soul
Takes flight, and, on the utmost brink
  Of yonder starry pole,
Discerns beyond the abyss of night
The dawn of uncreated light.

Night is the time to pray;
  Our Saviour oft withdrew
To desert mountains far away;
  So will his followers do,—
Steal from the throng to haunts untrod,
And commune there alone with God.

Night is the time for death;
  When all around is peace.
Calmly to yield the weary breath,
  From sin and suffering cease.
Think of Heaven's bliss, and give the sign
To parting friends:— such death be mine.

THE MILL-STREAM.

Long trails of cistus flowers
  Creep on the rocky hill :
And beds of strong spear-mint
  Grow round about the mill ;
And from a mountain tarn above,
  As peaceful as a dream,
Like to child unruly,
Though school'd and counsell'd truly,
  Foams down the wild mill-stream !

The wild mill-stream it dasheth,
  In merriment away,
And keeps the miller and his son
  So busy all the day!

Into the mad mill-stream
  The mountain roses fall;
And fern and adder's-tongue
  Grow on the old mill-wall.
The tarn is on the upland moor,
  Where not a leaf doth grow;
And through the mountain gashes
The merry mill-stream dashes
  Down to the sea below;
But in the quiet hollows
  The red trout groweth prime,
For the miller and the miller's son
  To angle when they 've time.

Then fair befall the stream
  That turns the mountain mill,
And fair befall the narrow road
  That windeth up the hill!
And good luck to the countryman,
  And to his old grey mare,
That upward toileth steadily,
With meal-sacks laden heavily,
  In storms as well as fair!
And good luck to the miller
  And to the miller's son;
And ever may the wind-wheel turn,
  While mountain waters run!

LOVE.

All thoughts, all passions, all delights,
Whatever stirs this mortal frame,
All are but ministers of Love,
  And feed his sacred flame.

Oft in my waking dreams do I
Live o'er again that happy hour,
When midway on the mount I lay
  Beside the ruin'd tower.

The moonshine, stealing o'er the scene,
Had blended with the lights of eve;
And she was there, my hope, my joy,
  My own dear Genevieve!

She lean'd against the armed man,
The statue of the armed knight;
She stood and listen'd to my lay
  Amid the lingering light.

Few sorrows hath she of her own,
My hope! my joy! my Genevieve!
She loves me best, whene'er I sing
  The songs that make her grieve.

I played a soft and doleful air,
I sang an old and moving story—
An old rude song that suited well
  That ruin wild and hoary.

She listen'd with a flitting blush,
With downcast eyes and modest grace;
For well she knew, I could not choose
   But gaze upon her face.

I told her of the Knight that wore
Upon his shield a burning brand;
And that for ten long years he woo'd
   The Lady of the Land.

I told her how he pined, and, ah!
The low, the deep, the pleading tone,
With which I sang another's love,
    Interpreted my own.

She listen'd with a flitting blush,
With downcast eyes, and modest grace;
And she forgave me that I gazed
    Too fondly on her face!

But when I told the cruel scorn
Which crazed this bold and lovely Knight,
And that he cross'd the mountain-woods,
    Nor rested day nor night;

That sometimes from the savage den,
And sometimes from the darksome shade,
And sometimes starting up at once
    In green and sunny glade,—

There came, and look'd him in the face,
An angel beautiful and bright;
And that he knew it was a Fiend,
    This miserable Knight!

And that, unknowing what he did,
He leap'd amid a murderous band,
And saved from outrage worse than death
    The Lady of the Land;

And how she wept and clasp'd his knees
And how she tended him in vain —
And ever strove to expiate
    The scorn that crazed his brain;

And that she nursed him in a cave;
And how his madness went away
When on the yellow forest-leaves
    A dying man he lay;

His dying words - but when I reach'd
That tenderest strain of all the ditty,
My faltering voice and pausing harp
  Disturb'd her soul with pity !

All impulses of soul and sense
Had thrill'd my guileless Genevieve,
The music and the doleful tale,
  The rich and balmy eve ;

And hopes, and fears that kindle hope,
An undistinguishable throng ;
And gentle wishes long subdued,
  Subdued and cherish'd long !

She wept with pity and delight,
She blush'd with love and virgin shame ;
And, like the murmur of a dream,
  I heard her breathe my name.

Her bosom heaved—she stept aside ;
As conscious of my look, she stept—
Then suddenly, with timorous eye
  She fled to me, and wept.

She half inclosed me with her arms,
She press'd me with a meek embrace ;
And, bending back her head, look'd up
  And gazed upon my face.

'Twas partly love, and partly fear,
And partly 'twas a bashful art
That I might rather feel, than see,
  The swelling of her heart.

I calm'd her fears ; and she was calm,
And told her love with virgin pride ;
And so I won my Genevieve,
  My bright and beauteous Bride !

FLOWERS OF THE FOREST.

I've seen the smiling
Of Fortune beguiling:
I've felt all its favours, and found its decay:
Sweet was its blessing,
Kind its caressing:
But now it is fled—it is fled far away.

I've seen the forest
Adorned the foremost
With flowers of the fairest most pleasant and gay;
Sae bonnie was their blooming!
Their scent the air perfuming!
But now they are wither'd and weded away.

I've seen the morning
With gold the hills adorning,
And loud tempest storming before the mid-day.

I've seen Tweed's silver streams
Shining in the sunny beams,
Grow drumly and dark as he row'd on his way.

Oh, fickle Fortune.
Why this cruel sporting?
Oh, why still perplex us, poor sons of a day?
Nae mair your smiles can cheer me,
Nae mair your frowns can fear me;
For the Flowers of the Forest are a' wede away.

YARROW UNVISITED.

FROM Stirling Castle we had seen
　The mazy Forth unravell'd;
Had trod the banks of Clyde, and Tay,
　And with the Tweed had travell'd;
And when we came to Clovenford,
　Then said my "winsome marrow,"
"Whate'er betide, we'll turn aside,
　And see the Braes of Yarrow."

"Let Yarrow folk, frae Selkirk Town,
　Who have been buying, selling,
Go back to Yarrow, 'tis their own;
　Each maiden to her dwelling!
On Yarrow's banks let herons feed,
　Hares couch, and rabbits burrow!
But we will downwards with the Tweed,
　Nor turn aside to Yarrow.

"There's Galla Water, Leader Haughs,
　Both lying right before us;
And Dryborough, where with chiming Tweed
　The lintwhites sing in chorus;
There's pleasant Tiviot-dale, a land
　Made blythe with plough and harrow:
Why throw away a needful day
　To go in search of Yarrow?

" What's Yarrow but a river bare,
    That glides the dark hills under?
There are a thousand such elsewhere
    As worthy of your wonder."
Strange words they seem'd of slight and scorn:
    My true-love sigh'd for sorrow,
And look'd me in the face, to think
    I thus could speak of Yarrow!

" Oh! green," said I, " are Yarrow's Holms,
    And sweet is Yarrow flowing!
Fair hangs the apple frae the rock,
    But we will leave it growing.
O'er hilly path, and open strath,
    We'll wander Scotland thorough;
But, though so near, we will not turn
    Into the Dale of Yarrow.

" Let beeves and home-bred kine partake
    The sweets of Burn-mill meadow:
The swan on still St. Mary's Lake
    Float double, swan and shadow!
We will not see them; will not go,
    To-day, nor yet to-morrow;
Enough, if in our hearts we know
    There's such a place as Yarrow.

" Be Yarrow Stream unseen, unknown!
    It must, or we shall rue it:
We have a vision of our own;
    Ah! why should we undo it?
The treasured dreams of times long past,
    We'll keep them, winsome marrow!
For when we're there, although 'tis fair,
    'Twill be another Yarrow!

" If Care with freezing years should come,
    And wandering seem but folly,—
Should we be loth to stir from home,
    And yet be melancholy ;
Should life be dull, and spirits low,
    'Twill soothe us in our sorrow,
That earth has something yet to show—
    The bonny Holms of Yarrow ! "

KING HENRY V. AND THE HERMIT
OF DREUX.

HE pass'd unquestion'd through the camp,
    Their heads the soldiers bent
In silent reverence, or begg'd
    A blessing as he went :
And so the Hermit pass'd along,
    And reach'd the royal tent.

King Henry sate in his tent alone,
    The map before him lay ;
Fresh conquests he was planning there
    To grace the future day.

King Henry lifted up his eyes
    The intruder to behold ;
With reverence he the Hermit saw,
    For the holy man was old.
His look was gentle as a Saint's,
    And yet his eye was bold.

" Repent thee, Henry, of the wrongs
    Which thou hast done this land !
O King, repent in time, for know
    The judgment is at hand.

" I have pass'd forty years of peace
    Beside the river Blaise,
But what a weight of woe hast thou
    Laid on my latter days!

" I used to see along the stream
    The white sail gliding down,
That wafted food in better times
    To yonder peaceful town.

" Henry! I never now behold
    The white sail gliding down;
Famine, Disease, and Death, and **Thou**
    Destroy that wretched town.

" I used to hear the traveller's voice
    As here he pass'd along,
Or maiden, as she loiter'd home,
    Singing her even-song.

" No traveller's voice may now be heard,
    In fear he hastens by;
But I have heard the village maid
    In vain for succour cry.

" I used to see the youths row down,
    And watch the dripping oar,
As pleasantly their viol's tones
    Came soften'd to the shore.

" King Henry, many a blacken'd corpse
    I now see floating down!
Thou man of blood! repent in time,
    And leave this 'leaguer'd town."

"I shall go on," King Henry cried.
 " And conquer this good land ;
  Seest thou not, Hermit, that the Lord
   Hath given it to my hand ?"

The Hermit heard King Henry speak,
 And angrily look'd down :
  His face was gentle, and for that
   More solemn was his frown.

" What if no miracle from Heaven
    The murderer's arm control,
Think you for that the weight of blood
    Lies lighter on his soul ?

" Thou conqueror King, repent in time,
    Or dread the coming woe !
For, Henry, thou hast heard the threat,
    And soon shalt feel the blow !"

King Henry forced a careless smile,
    As the Hermit went his way ;
But Henry soon remember'd him,
    Upon his dying day,

THE THREE FISHERMEN.

THREE fishers went sailing out into the West,
    Out into the West as the sun went down;
Each thought of the woman who loved him the best.
    And the children stood watching them out of the town:
        For men must work, and women must weep,
        And there's little to earn, and many to keep,
          Though the harbour-bar be moaning.

Three wives sat up in the lighthouse tower,
    And trimm'd the lamps as the sun went down,
And they look'd at the squall, and they look'd at the shower,
    And the rack it came rolling up, ragged and brown;
        But men must work, and women must weep,
        Though storms be sudden, and waters deep,
          And the harbour-bar be moaning.

Three corpses lay out on the shining sands,
    In the morning gleam, as the tide went down,
And the women are watching and wringing their hands,
    For those who will never come home to the town.

But men must work, and women must weep,
And the sooner it's over, the sooner to sleep,
And good-bye to the bar and its moaning.

YARROW VISITED.

And is this Yarrow?—*This* the stream
  Of which my fancy cherish'd,
So faithfully, a waking dream?
  An image that hath perish'd!
O that some minstrel's harp were near,
  To utter notes of gladness,
And chase this silence from the air,
  That fills my heart with sadness!

Yet why?—a silvery current flows,
  With uncontroll'd meanderings;
Nor have these eyes by greener hills
  Been soothed, in all my wanderings.
And, through her depths, St. Mary's Lake
  Is visibly delighted;
For not a feature of those hills
  Is in the mirror slighted.

A blue sky bends o'er Yarrow Vale,
  Save where that pearly whiteness
Is round the rising sun diffused,
  A tender, hazy brightness;
Mild dawn of promise! that excludes
  All profitless dejection;
Though not unwilling here to admit
  A pensive recollection.

Where was it that the famous Flower
   Of Yarrow Vale lay bleeding?
Its bed, perchance, was yon smooth mound
   On which the herd is feeding:
And haply from this crystal pool,
   Now peaceful as the morning.
The Water-wraith ascended thrice,
   And gave his doleful warning.

Delicious is the lay that sings
   The haunts of happy lovers.
The path that leads them to the grove,
   The leafy grove that covers:
And Pity sanctifies the verse
   That paints, by strength of sorrow,
The unconquerable strength of love;
   Bear witness, rueful Yarrow!

But thou, that didst appear so fair
   To fond imagination,
Dost rival in the light of day
   Her delicate creation:
Meek loveliness is round thee spread,
   A softness still and holy:
The grace of forest charms decay'd,
   And pastoral melancholy.

That region left, the Vale unfolds
   Rich groves of lofty stature,
With Yarrow winding through the pomp
   Of cultivated nature:
And, rising from those lofty groves,
   Behold a ruin hoary!
The shatter'd front of Newark's towers,
   Renown'd in Border story.

YARROW VISITED.

Fair scenes for childhood's opening bloom,
    For sportive youth to stray in;
For manhood to enjoy his strength;
    And age to wear away in!
Yon cottage seems a bower of bliss,
    A covert for protection
Of tender thoughts that nestle there,
    The brood of chaste affection.

How sweet, on this autumnal day,
    The wild-wood fruits to gather,
And on my true-love's forehead plant
    A crest of blooming heather!

And what if I enwreath'd my own!
  'Twere no offence to reason;
The sober hills thus deck their brows
  To meet the wintry season.

I see—but not by sight alone,
  Loved Yarrow, have I won thee!
A ray of fancy still survives—
  Her sunshine plays upon thee!
Thy ever youthful waters keep
  A course of lively pleasure;
And gladsome notes my lips can breathe,
  Accordant to the measure.

The vapours linger round the heights,
  They melt—and soon must vanish;
One hour is theirs, nor more is mine—
  Sad thought, which I would banish,
But that I know, where'er I go,
  Thy genuine image, Yarrow!
Will dwell with me—to heighten joy,
  And cheer my mind in sorrow.

JOCK O' HAZELDEAN.

" Why weep ye by the tide, ladye?
    Why weep ye by the tide?
I 'll wed ye to my youngest son,
    And ye shall be his bride;
And ye shall be his bride, ladye,
    Sae comely to be seen :"
But aye she loot the tears down fa'
    For Jock o' Hazeldean.

" Now let this wilfu' grief be done,
    And dry that cheek so pale ;
Young Frank is chief of Errington,
    And lord of Langley-dale ;
His step is first in peaceful ha',
    His sword in battle keen :"
But aye she loot the tears down fa'
    For Jock o' Hazeldean.

" A chain of gold ye sall not lack,
    Nor braid to bind your hair,
Nor mettled hound, nor managed hawk,
    Nor palfrey fresh and fair ;
And you, the foremost o' them a',
    Shall ride our forest queen :"
But aye she loot the tears down fa'
    For Jock o' Hazeldean.

The kirk was deck'd at morning-tide,
　The tapers glimmer'd fair;
The priest and bridegroom wait the bride,
　And dame and knight are there:
They sought her baith by bower and ha';
　The ladye was not seen!
She's o'er the Border, and awa'
　Wi' Jock o' Hazeldean.

THE STORMY PETREL.

A THOUSAND miles from land are we,
Tossing about on the roaring sea;
From billow to bounding billow cast,
Like fleecy snow on the stormy blast:
The sails are scatter'd abroad, like weeds,
The strong masts shake like quivering reeds.

The mighty cables, and iron chains,
The hull, which all earthly strength disdains,
They strain and they crack, and hearts like stone,
Their natural, hard, proud strength disown.

Up and down! up and down!
From the base of the wave to the billow's crown,
And amidst the flashing and feathery foam,
The Stormy Petrel finds a home,—
A home, if such a place may be,
For her who lives on the wide, wide sea,
On the craggy ice, in the frozen air,
And only seeketh her rocky lair
To warm her young, and to teach them spring
At once o'er the waves on the stormy wing.

O'er the deep! o'er the deep!
Where the whale, and the shark, and the sword-fish sleep,
Outflying the blast and the driving rain,
The Petrel telleth her tale, in vain
For the mariner curseth the warning bird,
That bringeth him news of the storm unheard.
Ah! thus doth the prophet of good or ill,
Meet hate from the creature he serveth still:
Yet he ne'er falters—so, Petrel, spring
Once more o'er the waves on thy stormy wing!

THE BREEZE IN THE CHURCH

'Twas a sunny day, and the morning psalm
　　We sang in the church together;
We felt in our hearts the joy and calm
　　Of the calm and joyous weather.

The slow, and sweet, and sacred strain,
　　Through every bosom stealing,
Check'd every thought that was light and vain,
　　And waked each holy feeling.

We knew by its sunny gleam how clear
　　Was the blue sky smiling o'er us,
And in every pause in the hymn could hear
　　The wild birds' happy chorus.

And lo! from its haunts by cave or rill
　　With a sudden start awaking,
A breeze came fluttering down the hill,
　　Its fragrant pinions shaking.

Through the open windows it bent its way,
　　And down the chancel's centre,
Like a privileged thing that at will might stray,
　　And in holy places enter.

From niche to niche, from nook to nook,
　　With a lightsome rustle flying,
It lifted the leaves of the Holy Book,
　　On the altar-cushion lying.

THE BREEZE IN THE CHURCH.

It fann'd the old clerk's hoary hair,
   And the children's bright young faces;
Then vanish'd, none knew how or where,
   Leaving its pleasant traces.

It left sweet thoughts of summer hours
   Spent on the quiet mountains;
And the church seem'd full of the scent of flowers,
   And the trickling fall of fountains.

The image of scenes so still and fair
   With our music sweetly blended,
While it seem'd their whisper'd hymn took share
   In the praise that to heaven ascended.

We thought of Him who had pour'd the rills,
   And through the green mountains led them,
Whose hand, when He piled the enduring hills,
   With a mantle of beauty spread them.

And a purer passion was borne above,
   In a louder anthem swelling,
As we bow'd to the visible Spirit of Love,
   On those calm summits dwelling.

THE BALLAD OF THE BEAR-HUNTERS.

THREE hunters went a-hunting
  In wild woods far away,
To chase the bear on mountain slopes
  At dawning of the day.
They met Dame Joris on the road,
  Plump as a gourd was she,
And with her went her daughter bright,
  The rose-red Margerie.
      And it's whoop! Oho! Hollo! Hallò!
        The morn is shining fair.
      Whoop! Hollo! Hey! and wish us joy,
        A-hunting of the bear.

"Get supper for us, Joris,
  When we return to-night;
Good beer and wine, and crackling chine,
  And a fire-side warm and bright.
Ere sets the sun, three hungry men,
  We'll seek your hostelry;
And Bruin dead in his old grey coat
  Shall bear us company.

For it's whoop! Oho! Hollo! Hallò!
　　The morn is shining fair.
Whoop! Hollo! Hoy! and wish us joy,
　　A-hunting of the bear."

"I've got," quo' she, "a ven'son haunch,
　　A turkey served with brawn,
And foaming flagons of wine as good
　　As ever from cask was drawn.
And if you slay the shaggy bear
　　That prowls our forests through,
I'll find the meat, and share the drink,
　　And charge you ne'er a sou.
　　　　For it's whoop! Oho! Hollo! Hallò!
　　　　　　The morn is shining fair.
　　　　Whoop! Hollo! Hoy! I wish you joy,
　　　　　　A-hunting of the bear."

"What wilt *thou* give us, maiden?"
　　Said Reinhold, whispering low,
And clasp'd her by the yielding hand,
　　That nobody might know.
"I wish for something better than wine,
　　Better than golden fee,—
A look, a smile, or word of love,
　　From rose-red Margerie.
　　　　For it's whoop! Oho! Hollo! Hallò!
　　　　　　The morn is shining fair.
　　　　Whoop! Hollo! Hoy! and wish me joy,
　　　　　　A-hunting of the bear."

173

"I'll give," quo' she, "a squeezing hand
　　When nobody is nigh,
A whisper'd word, a favouring smile,
　　A twinkle of the eye.
I'll give;—but what have I to give,
　　Although I speak so free,
Unless it be a vow of truth,
　　And the heart of Margerie?
　　　　For it's whoop! Oho! Hollo! Hallo!
　　　　　The morn is shining fair.
　　　　Whoop! Hollo! Hoy! I wish you joy,
　　　　　A-hunting of the bear."

They had their hunting on the hill,
　　And merry men were they;
And a beaten foe was Bruin the bold,
　　At closing of the day.
And Joris spread a regal feast,—
　　The ven'son and the chine,
Turkey and brawn, and snow-white cheese,
　　And overflowing wine.
　　　　And 'twas whoop! Oho! Hollo! Hallo!
　　　　　The wine-cup circles fair.
　　　　Whoop! Hollo! Hoy! 'tis ever joy,
　　　　　A-hunting of the bear.

"We track'd his steps an hour ere noon—
　　'Twas up amid the snow;
And then we track'd him down again,
　　To his rocky dells below

"And then our shots—one—two—and three—
    Went whizzing in his side;
    And the echoes raised a thunder tone,
    As he howl'd his last, and died.
        And 'tis whoop! Oho! Hollo! Hallô!
        The wine-cup circles fair.
        Whoop! Hollo! Hoy! 'tis ever joy,
        A-hunting of the bear."

And Reinhold pledged his maiden bright
  Again and yet again:
"I've woo'd thee, Margerie, many a month,—
  Oh, help me out of pain!"
"There, take my hand," said Margerie fair,
  "And wed me, while you can;
But go no more a-hunting,
  When you're a married man.

    For his whoop! Oho! Hollo! Hallo!
      The bachelor may care;
    But married men should stay at home
      From the hunting of the bear."

I WANDERED BY THE BROOK-SIDE.

I WANDERED by the brook-side,
  I wandered by the mill,—
I could not hear the brook flow,
  The noisy wheel was still;
There was no burr of grasshopper,
  No chirp of any bird,
But the beating of my own heart
  Was all the sound I heard.

I sat beside the elm-tree,
  I watch'd the long, long shade,
And, as it grew still longer,
  I did not feel afraid;
For I listen'd for a footfall,
  I listen'd for a word,—
But the beating of my own heart
  Was all the sound I heard.

He came not, no, he came not,
The night came on alone,
The little stars sat one by one,
Each on a golden throne;

The evening air pass'd by my cheek,
  The leaves above were stirr'd,
But the beating of my own heart
  Was all the sound I heard.

Fast silent tears were flowing,
  When something stood behind.
A hand was on my shoulder,
  I knew its touch was kind:
It drew me nearer—nearer,—
  We did not speak one word,
For the beating of our own hearts
  Was all the sound we heard.

THE BATTLE OF BLENHEIM

It was a summer evening,
  Old Kaspar's work was done,
And he before his cottage door
  Was sitting in the sun,
And by him sported on the green
His little grandchild Wilhelmine.

She saw her brother Peterkin
  Roll something large and round,
Which he beside the rivulet
  In playing there had found;
He came to ask what he had found,
That was so large, and smooth, and round.

Old Kaspar took it from the boy,
  Who stood expectant by;
And then the old man shook his head,
  And, with a natural sigh,
" 'Tis some poor fellow's skull," said he,
" Who fell in the great victory.

" I find them in the garden,
  For there's many here about;
And often when I go to plough,
  The ploughshare turns them out
For many thousand men," said he,
" Were slain in that great victory."

" Now tell us what 'twas all about,"
    Young Peterkin he cries ;
And little Wilhelmine looks up
    With wonder-waiting eyes ;
" Now tell us all about the war,
And what they fought each other for."

" It was the English, Kaspar cried,
    " Who put the French to rout
But what they fought each other for,
    I could not well make out ;
But everybody said," quoth he,
" That 'twas a famous victory.

" My father lived at Blenheim then,
    Yon little stream hard by ;
They burnt his dwelling to the ground,
    And he was forced to fly :
So with his wife and child he fled,
Nor had he where to rest his head.

" With fire and sword the country round
    Was wasted far and wide,
And many a childing mother then,
    And new-born baby died ;
But things like that, you know, must be
At every famous victory.

" They say it was a shocking sight
    After the field was won ;
For many thousand bodies here
    Lay rotting in the sun ;
But things like that, you know, must be
After a famous victory.

"Great praise the Duke of Marlbro' won,
   And our good Prince Eugene."
"Why 'twas a very wicked thing!"
   Said little Wilhelmine.
"Nay, nay, my little girl," quoth he,
"It was a famous victory.

"And everybody praised the Duke
   Who this great fight did win."
"But what good came of it at last?"
   Quoth little Peterkin.
"Why, that I cannot tell," said he,
"But 'twas a famous victory."

THINK OF ME.

Go where the water glideth gently ever,
  Glideth through meadows that the greenest be ;
Go, listen to your own beloved river,
    And think of me !

Wander in forests, where the small flower layeth
  Its fairy gem beneath the giant tree ;
List to the dim brook pining as it playeth,
    And think of me !

And when the sky is silver-pale at even,
  And the wind grieveth in the lonely tree,
Go out beneath the solitary heaven,
    And think of me!

And when the moon riseth, as she were dreaming,
  And treadeth with white feet the lulled sea,
Go, silent as a star, beneath her beaming,
    And think of me!

www.ingramcontent.com/pod-product-compliance
Lightning Source LLC
Chambersburg PA
CBHW020538270326
41927CB00006B/631